PREFACE

1. Scope

This publication provides joint doctrine for the command and control of joint air operations across the range of military operations.

2. Purpose

This publication has been prepared under the direction of the Chairman of the Joint Chiefs of Staff (CJCS). It sets forth joint doctrine to govern the activities and performance of the Armed Forces of the United States in joint operations and provides the doctrinal basis for US military coordination with other US Government departments and agencies during operations and for US military involvement in multinational operations. It provides military guidance for the exercise of authority by combatant commanders and other joint force commanders (JFCs) and prescribes joint doctrine for operations, education, and training. It provides military guidance for use by the Armed Forces in preparing their appropriate plans. It is not the intent of this publication to restrict the authority of the JFC from organizing the force and executing the mission in a manner the JFC deems most appropriate to ensure unity of effort in the accomplishment of the overall objective.

3. Application

a. Joint doctrine established in this publication applies to the joint staff, commanders of combatant commands, subunified commands, joint task forces, subordinate components of these commands, the Services, and combat support agencies.

b. The guidance in this publication is authoritative; as such, this doctrine will be followed except when, in the judgment of the commander, exceptional circumstances dictate otherwise. If conflicts arise between the contents of this publication and the contents of Service publications, this publication will take precedence unless the CJCS, normally in coordination with the other members of the Joint Chiefs of Staff, has provided more current and specific guidance. Commanders of forces operating as part of a multinational (alliance or coalition) military command should follow multinational doctrine and procedures ratified by the United States. For doctrine and procedures not ratified by the United States, commanders should evaluate and follow the multinational command's doctrine and procedures, where applicable and consistent with US law, regulations, and doctrine.

For the Chairman of the Joint Chiefs of Staff

DAVID L. GOLDFEIN, Lt Gen, USAF
Director, Joint Staff

Intentionally Blank

- Adds a discussion of mission command as it relates to joint air operations and the concept of centralized control and decentralized execution.

- Clarifies the command authorities of the joint force air component commander (JFACC) and considerations for allocation of air forces.

- Updates and clarifies considerations and options for designation of a JFACC at the theater and/or sub-theater level.

- Updates the description of the airspace control authority and airspace control considerations.

- Updates descriptions of the Service elements of the theater air-ground system, to include addition of command and control (C2) of special operations air forces.

- Adds a description of the Navy composite warfare commander approach to C2.

- Updates the discussion of unmanned aircraft system planning considerations and operations.

- Adds sections on C2 of air operations during defense support to civil authorities and homeland defense; air operations in a chemical, biological, radiological, and nuclear environment; operations near international borders; and C2 of space forces.

- Updates the description of the targeting process and the joint air tasking cycle.

- Expands the discussion of the joint air component coordination element.

- Removes Appendix E, "Sample Airspace Control Plan."

- Assumes proponency for the term "unmanned aircraft system."

- Modifies the terms "air and space expeditionary task force" and "air and space operations center" and the definitions of "air tasking order," "allocation request," and "unmanned aircraft."

- Removes the terms "allotment," "tactical air support element," and "traffic pattern."

Intentionally Blank

TABLE OF CONTENTS

Intentionally Blank

EXECUTIVE SUMMARY
COMMANDER'S OVERVIEW

- **Provides an Introduction to Command and Control for Joint Air Operations**

- **Describes Establishing and Exercising Command and Control of Joint Air Operations**

- **Explains Planning and Execution of Joint Air Operations**

Introduction

The joint force commander's (JFC's) air component should be organized for coordinated action through unity of command using the air capabilities of the joint force.

Historically, control of the air has been a prerequisite to success for modern operations or campaigns because it prevents enemy air and missile threats from effectively interfering with operations of friendly air, land, maritime, space, and special operations forces, facilitating freedom of action and movement. Joint air operations are normally conducted using centralized control and decentralized execution to achieve effective control and foster initiative, responsiveness, and flexibility.

Command and Control of Joint Air Operations

Joint Force Commander

When contemplating command and control (C2) options for joint air operations within the operational area, the joint force commander (JFC) can choose to exercise C2 through a functional component commander by designating a joint force air component commander (JFACC), one of the Service component commanders, or the joint force staff. Many factors will weigh on the JFC's selection—most notably the type and availability of forces and capabilities to accomplish the assigned mission.

Joint Force Air Component Commander

The JFC normally designates a joint force air component commander (JFACC) to establish unity of command and unity of effort for joint air operations.

The JFC will normally assign JFACC responsibilities to the component commander having the preponderance of forces to be tasked and the ability to effectively plan, task, and control joint air operations. However, the JFC will always consider the mission, nature, and duration of the operation, force capabilities, and the C2 capabilities in selecting a commander. The responsibilities of the JFACC are assigned by the JFC. These include, but are not limited to:

- Develop a joint air operations plan (JAOP);

- Recommend to the JFC air apportionment priorities;

- Allocate and task the joint air capabilities and forces made available by the Service components based on the JFC's air apportionment decision;

- Provide the JFACC's guidance in the air operations directive (AOD) for the use of joint air capabilities for a specified period that is used throughout the planning stages of the joint air tasking cycle and the execution of the air tasking order (ATO);

- Perform the duties of the airspace control authority (ACA), if designated;

- Perform the duties of the area air defense commander (AADC), if designated; and

- Perform the duties of the space coordinating authority (SCA), if designated.

Airspace Control Authority   The ACA is a commander designated by the JFC to assume overall responsibility for the operation of the airspace control system in the airspace control area. Developed by the ACA and approved by the JFC, the airspace control plan establishes general guidance for the control of airspace and procedures for the airspace control system for the joint force operational area.

Area Air Defense Commander   The AADC is responsible for defensive counterair (DCA) operations, which include the integrated air defense system for the joint operations area. DCA and offensive counterair operations combine as the counterair mission, which is designed to attain and maintain the degree of air superiority desired by the JFC. In coordination with the component commanders, the AADC develops, integrates, and distributes a JFC-approved joint area air defense plan.

Joint Air Operations Command and Control System   The C2 system for joint air operations will vary depending on the operational area and specific missions. Whether it is the Air Force's theater air control system, the Army air-ground system, the Navy's composite warfare commander/Navy tactical air control system, Marine air command and control system, or the special operations air-ground system that serves as the nucleus for C2 of joint air operations, the remainder will be integrated to best support the JFC's concept of operations (CONOPS).

Joint Force Air Component Command Organization

A joint air operations center (JAOC) provides the capability to plan, coordinate, allocate, task, execute, monitor, and assess the activities of assigned or attached forces.

The JFACC will normally operate from a joint air operations center (JAOC). The JAOC is structured to operate as a fully integrated command center and should be staffed by members of all participating components, to include key staff positions, in order to fulfill the JFACC's responsibilities. Elements that should be common to all JAOCs are the strategy division, combat plans division, intelligence, surveillance, and reconnaissance (ISR) division, air mobility division (AMD), and combat operations division.

Joint Force Staff Option

In operations of limited scope, duration, or complexity, or in which air operations are a relatively small aspect of the overall joint force, the JFC may plan, direct, and control joint air operations with the assistance of the JFC staff. In this situation, the JFC would retain command authority and responsibility and would normally request augmentation from appropriate components to perform the C2 air function and assist in planning and coordinating joint air operations.

Liaisons

Each component normally provides liaison elements that work within the JAOC.

In addition to the JFC and staff, other component commanders and their staffs require continuous and ready access to the JFACC and the JFACC's staff. Principal means of accomplishing this is through personal contact, the established communications and information support system, and liaison personnel. These liaisons work for their respective component commanders and work with the JFACC and staff.

Joint Force Air Component Commander Basing and Transition

Effective joint air operations planning must contain provisions to transition JFACC responsibilities

In large-scale air operations, land-based JFACCs and JAOCs are normally desired because of the enhanced logistics and communications provided by additional equipment and workspaces that may not be available on sea-based facilities. The JFACC and JAOC may be sea-based when any one of the following conditions are present:

- Maritime forces provide the preponderance of air assets and have the organizational construct, operating experience, and management functions capability to effectively plan, task, and control joint air operations.

between components of the joint force and/or JFC's staff. The JFACC transition should be identified in the joint air operations plan.	• Land-based facilities or sufficient infrastructure does not exist. • A secure land-based area is not available, and ground support forces are forced to withdraw.
Command and Control of Joint Air Operations for Defense Support of Civil Authorities and Homeland Defense	Commander, United States Northern Command and Commander, United States Pacific Command share the primary mission for US homeland defense and defense support of civil authorities within their assigned areas of responsibility (AORs).

Planning and Execution of Joint Air Operations

Joint Air Operations Planning	The JFC's estimate of the operational environment and articulation of the objectives needed to accomplish the mission form the basis for determining components' objectives. The JFACC uses the JFC's mission, commander's estimate and objectives, commander's intent, CONOPS, and the components' objectives to develop a course of action (COA). When the JFC approves the JFACC's COA, it becomes the basis for more detailed joint air operations planning—expressing what, where, and how joint air operations will affect the adversary or current situation.
The Joint Air Estimate	The joint air estimate is described as a process of reasoning by which the air component commander considers all the circumstances affecting the military situation and decides on a COA to be taken to accomplish the mission. The joint air estimate reflects the JFACC's analysis of the various COAs that may be used to accomplish the assigned mission(s) and contains the recommendation for the best COA.
The Joint Operation Planning Process for Air	The JFACC is responsible for planning joint air operations and uses the joint operation planning process for air (JOPPA) to develop a JAOP that guides employment of the air capabilities and forces made available to accomplish missions assigned by the JFC. JOPPA follows the joint operation planning process found in Joint Publication 5-0, *Joint Operation Planning*, with specific details for joint air operations. JOPPA drives the production of the JAOP and supporting plans and orders.
Joint Targeting	The JFC will normally delegate the authority to conduct execution planning, coordination, and deconfliction

associated with joint air targeting to the JFACC and will ensure that this process is a joint effort. Targets scheduled for attack by component air capabilities and forces should be included on an ATO for deconfliction and coordination.

The Targeting Effects Team

The JFACC may establish a targeting effects team (TET) as part of the JAOC. The TET validates targets to be engaged by joint air forces per the JFC's targeting guidance, links targets to appropriate tactical tasks in the AOD, weaponeers targets to create desired effects, and verifies measures of effectiveness/measures of performance.

The Joint Air Tasking Cycle

The joint air tasking cycle process provides an iterative, cyclic process for the planning, apportionment, allocation, coordination, and tasking of joint air missions and sorties within the guidance of the JFC. The joint air tasking cycle is synchronized with the JFC's battle rhythm. The full joint air tasking cycle, from JFC guidance to the start of ATO execution, is dependent on the JFC's and JFACC's procedures. The precise timeframes should be specified in the JFC's operation plan or the JFACC's JAOP.

Intelligence, Surveillance, and Reconnaissance Considerations

The JFC will normally delegate collection operations management for joint airborne ISR to the JFACC to authoritatively direct, schedule, and control collection operations for use by the J-2 [intelligence directorate of a joint staff] in associated processing, exploitation, and reporting. The JAOC should request ISR support from the JFC or another component if available assets cannot fulfill specific airborne ISR requirements.

Air Mobility Considerations

Airlift is critical for deployment, redeployment, airdrop, aeromedical evacuation, and sustainment, while aerial refueling is critical to deployment, redeployment, sustainment, and employment of air operations.

Integrating air mobility planning into the JAOP and monitoring mission execution is normally the responsibility of the AMD chief supported by a team of mobility specialists in the JAOC. Intratheater airlift and theater refueling assets may be attached to a joint task force, with operational control normally delegated down to the appropriate Service component commander (usually the commander, Air Force forces). The director of mobility forces (DIRMOBFOR) is normally a senior officer who is familiar with the AOR and possesses an extensive background in air mobility operations. Operationally, the DIRMOBFOR exercises coordinating authority for air mobility with commands and agencies within and external to the joint force. Specifically, the DIRMOBFOR coordinates with the JFACC's JAOC, Air Mobility

Command's 618 Operations Center Tanker Airlift Control Center, and joint movement center/joint deployment and distribution operations center to expedite the resolution of air mobility issues.

Unmanned Aircraft Systems Considerations

Unmanned aircraft systems (UASs) should be treated similarly to manned systems with regard to the established doctrinal warfighting principles. Several characteristics of UASs can make C2 particularly challenging:

- UAS communication links are generally more critical than those required for manned systems.

- UASs may be capable of transferring control of the aircraft and/or payloads to multiple operators while airborne.

- Most larger UASs have considerably longer endurance times than comparable manned systems.

- Compliance with the airspace control order is critical. Unlike manned aircraft, UASs cannot typically "see and avoid" other aircraft.

Personnel Recovery Considerations

Since personnel recovery (PR) often relies on air assets to accomplish some of the PR execution tasks, coordination between the joint personnel recovery center (JPRC) and JAOC is essential. The JPRC is responsible for providing the information that goes into the PR portion of the ATO special instructions.

Command and Control of Space Forces

Space forces typically operate in general or direct support to other JFCs. Geographic combatant commanders may designate a SCA and delegate appropriate authorities for planning and integrating space requirements and support for the theater.

CONCLUSION

This publication provides joint doctrine for the command and control of joint air operations across the range of military operations.

CHAPTER I
INTRODUCTION

"The lesson from the last war that stands out clearly above all the others is that if you want to go anywhere in modern war, in the air, on the sea, on the land, you must have command of the air."

**Fleet Admiral William F. "Bull" Halsey, Jr.,
Testimony to Congress following WWII**

1. General

This publication provides joint doctrine for the command and control (C2) of joint air operations and discusses the responsibilities of a joint force air component commander (JFACC). C2 is established by the joint force commander (JFC) through command relationships among subordinate commanders as described in Joint Publication (JP) 1, *Doctrine for the Armed Forces of the United States,* and JP 3-0, *Joint Operations.* Although the JFC has several organizational options for C2 of joint air operations, a JFACC is often the first option for consideration.

a. **Air Domain.** The air domain is described as the atmosphere, beginning at the Earth's surface, extending to the altitude where its effects upon operations become negligible. While domains are useful constructs for visualizing and characterizing the physical environment in which operations are conducted (the operational area), the use of the term "domain" is not meant to imply or mandate exclusivity, primacy, or C2 of any domain. Specific authorities and responsibilities within an operational area are as specified by the appropriate JFC.

b. **Control of the Air.** Historically, control of the air has been a prerequisite to success for modern operations or campaigns because it prevents enemy air and missile threats from effectively interfering with operations of friendly air, land, maritime, space, and special operations forces (SOF), facilitating freedom of action and movement. Dominance of the air cannot be assumed. In the air, the degree of control can range from no control, to a parity (or neutral) situation wherein neither adversary can claim any level of control over the other, to local air superiority in a specific area, to air supremacy over the entire operational area. Control may vary over time. It is important to remember that the degree of control of the air lies within a spectrum that can be enjoyed by any combatant. Likewise, that degree of control can be localized geographically (horizontally and vertically), or defined in the context of an entire theater. The desired degree of control will be at the direction of the JFC and based on the JFC's concept of operations (CONOPS), and will typically be an initial priority objective of joint air operations.

c. Commanders at all levels should consider how space, cyberspace, and information-related capabilities can affect the effectiveness and execution of joint air operations. Proper recognition and integration of these force capabilities during planning and execution is essential.

> *"The inherent flexibility of air power is its greatest asset. This flexibility makes it possible to employ the whole weight of the available air power against selected areas in turn; such concentrated use of the air striking force is a battle winning factor of the first importance. Control of available air power must be centralized and command must be exercised through the air force commander if this inherent flexibility and ability to deliver a decisive blow are to be fully exploited."*
>
> **Field Manual 100-20, Command and Employment of Air Power 1943**

2. Organization of Forces

a. JFCs organize forces to accomplish the mission based on their intent and CONOPS, developed in coordination with their component commanders and supporting organizations. Sound organization should provide for unity of command, centralized planning and direction, and decentralized execution, and be sufficiently flexible to meet the planned phases of the contemplated operation. JFCs provide direction and guidance to subordinate commanders and establish command relationships to enable effective spans of control, responsiveness, tactical flexibility, and protection.

b. The JFC's air component should be organized for coordinated action through unity of command using the air capabilities of the joint force. Centralized control and decentralized execution are key C2 considerations when organizing for joint air operations. While JFCs have full authority, within establishing directives, to assign missions, redirect efforts, and direct coordination among subordinate commanders, they should allow Service tactical and operational groupings to generally function as they were designed. The intent is to meet the needs of the JFC while maintaining the tactical and operational integrity of the Service organizations.

See JP 3-0, Joint Operations, for further discussion on the organization of joint forces.

c. A JFC has three basic organizational options for C2 of joint air operations: designate a JFACC, designate a Service component commander, or retain C2. In each case, effectively and efficiently organizing the staff, C2 systems, and subordinate forces that will plan, execute, and assess joint air operations is key. Factors impacting selection of each option may include the overall mission, forces available, the ability to C2, and the desired span of control.

d. **When designated, the JFACC is the commander** within a combatant command, subordinate unified command, or joint task force (JTF) responsible for tasking joint air forces, planning and coordinating joint air operations, or accomplishing such operational missions as may be assigned. The JFACC is given the authority necessary to accomplish missions and tasks assigned by the establishing commander.

See Chapter II, "Command and Control of Joint Air Operations," for further detailed discussion of JFC options for C2 of joint air operations and the roles and responsibilities of the JFACC.

3. Joint Air Operations

a. Joint air operations are performed by forces made available for joint air tasking. Joint air operations do not include those air operations that a component conducts as an integral and organic part of its own operations. Though missions vary widely within the operational environment and across the range of military operations, the framework and process for the conduct of joint air operations must be consistent.

b. **Joint air operations are normally conducted using centralized control and decentralized execution** to achieve effective control and foster initiative, responsiveness, and flexibility. In joint air operations centralized control is giving one commander the responsibility and authority for planning, directing, and coordinating a military operation or group/category of operations. Centralized control facilitates the integration of forces for the joint air effort and maintains the ability to focus the impact of joint air forces as needed throughout the operational area. **Decentralized execution** is the delegation of execution authority to subordinate commanders. This makes it possible to generate the required tempo of operations and to cope with the uncertainty, disorder, and fluidity of combat.

(1) **Mission Command.** Mission command is the conduct of military operations through decentralized execution based upon mission-type orders and is a key component of the C2 function. Its intent is for subordinates to clearly understand the commander's intent and to foster flexibility and initiative at the tactical level to best accomplish the mission. While philosophically consistent with historical C2 of air operations, modern joint air operations and their unique aspects of speed, range, and flexibility demand a balanced approach to C2. This approach is best codified in centralized control and decentralized execution.

(2) The specific missions and capabilities will drive the level of centralized control required for joint air operations, and the extent that mission-type orders may be used. Close air support (CAS) and personnel recovery (PR) missions typically have a high degree of uncertainty and complexity, and therefore require greater latitude in mission tasking and a higher degree of decentralized execution. Highly sensitive strike missions against long-range strategic targets will generally require a higher level of detailed planning and centralized control.

(3) Over-controlling joint air operations can reduce tactical flexibility, taking away initiative from operators. Insufficient guidance may result in failure to capitalize on joint force integration or may degrade operational-level flexibility, such as shifting JFC priorities, thus reducing effectiveness. A balanced approach to C2 of joint air operations using centralized control and decentralized execution, which is consistent with mission command, can best meet the needs of the JFC.

See JP 3-31, Command and Control for Joint Land Operations, *for additional discussion of mission command.*

c. Because joint air operations for a particular operation or campaign are often conducted theater-wide, the JFC will normally delegate some theater-wide authorities and responsibilities to the air component. To ensure proper force integration, all Service and functional components must support the development of the joint air operations plan (JAOP). This includes adherence to the JFC's approved guidance provided by the rules of engagement (ROE), airspace control plan (ACP), the airspace control order (ACO), the area air defense plan (AADP), and the special instructions (SPINS) located in the air tasking order (ATO). This will greatly aid in maximizing combat effectiveness, minimizing the risk of friendly fire and collateral damage, assuring deconfliction, and achieving the JFC's overall objectives.

d. Joint air operations may be complicated by civilian use of airspace, coordination with other United States Government (USG) departments and agencies, intergovernmental organizations (IGOs), and nongovernmental organizations (NGOs), or integration of host nation or multinational air forces. For example, joint air operations may be hindered by an inadequate host nation airspace control structure, which may result in the need for one to be established by the joint force. Close coordination, deconfliction, and liaison with all participating military, government, and nonmilitary and non-US entities are essential to effect unity of effort in the conduct of joint air operations.

See Chapter III, "Planning and Execution of Joint Air Operations," for further detailed discussion of the processes and products for planning and executing joint air operations.

CHAPTER II
COMMAND AND CONTROL OF JOINT AIR OPERATIONS

"If we lose the war in the air, we lose the war and we lose it quickly."

Field Marshal Bernard Montgomery, 1887-1976

SECTION A. ESTABLISHING COMMAND AND CONTROL

1. Joint Force Commander

a. **Authority.** The JFC has the authority to organize both assigned and attached forces to best accomplish the assigned mission based on the CONOPS. The JFC establishes subordinate commands, assigns responsibilities, establishes or delegates appropriate command relationships, and establishes coordinating instructions for subordinate commanders. When organizing joint forces, simplicity and clarity are critical.

See JP 1, Doctrine for the Armed Forces of the United States, *for additional doctrinal guidance on command relationships.*

b. **C2 Options.** When contemplating C2 options for joint air operations within the operational area, the JFC can choose to exercise C2 through a functional component commander by designating a JFACC, one of the Service component commanders, or the joint force staff. Many factors will weigh on the JFC's selection—most notably the type and availability of forces and capabilities to accomplish the assigned mission. Other factors for consideration in determining which C2 option to use include:

(1) **Span of control** is the JFC's ability to effectively manage the actions of subordinates. Span of control is based on the number of subordinates, number of activities, range of weapon systems, force capabilities, and the size and complexity of the operational area.

(2) When **joint air operations are the only operations or the duration and scope of air operations are of a very limited nature,** the JFC may elect to plan, direct, and control joint air operations through the joint forces staff.

(3) **Expertise** in effective and efficient employment of joint air assets to accomplish the JFC's mission is available. If the JFC elects to conduct joint air operations through the joint staff, the staff must be properly manned and adequately equipped with both the personnel expertise and the C2 equipment and processes necessary to direct and control the joint air effort.

(4) **Complexity and Scope of Joint Air Operations.** If the scope or complexity of the operations is significant, the JFC should consider designating a JFACC. This will allow the JFC time to focus on the overall campaign vice spending it on directing air operations.

c. **Theater-Level Considerations.** The geographic combatant commander (GCC) will weigh the operational circumstances and decide if available air forces/capabilities can be most effectively employed at the GCC level, the subordinate JFC level, or some combination thereof. This decision requires careful consideration after a thorough dialogue among the joint and Service component/force commanders.

2. Joint Force Air Component Commander

a. **Designation. The JFC normally designates a JFACC to establish unity of command and unity of effort for joint air operations.** The JFC will normally assign JFACC responsibilities to the component commander having the preponderance of forces to be tasked and the ability to effectively plan, task, and control joint air operations. **However the JFC will always consider the mission, nature, and duration of the operation, force capabilities, and the C2 capabilities in selecting a commander.**

b. **Authority.** The JFC delegates the JFACC the authority necessary to accomplish assigned missions and tasks. The JFACC will normally exercise tactical control (TACON) over forces made available for tasking. Service component commanders will normally retain operational control (OPCON) over their assigned and attached Service forces. Since the JFC will normally designate one of the Service component commanders as the JFACC, the dual-designated Service component commander/JFACC will exercise OPCON over their own Service forces as the Service component commander and TACON over other Services' forces made available for tasking. The JFC may also establish support relationships between the JFACC and other components to facilitate operations. **The JFACC conducts joint air operations in accordance with the JFC's intent and CONOPS.**

c. The JFC may designate the JFACC as the supported commander for strategic attack, air interdiction, PR, and airborne intelligence, surveillance, and reconnaissance (ISR) (among other missions). As such, the JFACC is responsible to the JFC for planning, coordinating, executing, and assessing these missions. Other component commanders may support the JFACC in accomplishing these missions, subject to the demands of their own JFC-assigned missions or as explicitly directed by the JFC. Normally, the JFACC is the supported commander for the JFC's overall air interdiction effort and the land and maritime forces commanders (e.g., joint force land component commander [JFLCC], joint force maritime component commander [JFMCC]) are supported commanders for interdiction in their designated area of operation (AO) and have the authority to designate target priority, effects, and timing of fires within their AOs.

d. **Responsibilities.** The responsibilities of the JFACC are assigned by the JFC. These include, but are not limited to:

(1) **Develop a JAOP** to best support the JFC's CONOPS or operation plan (OPLAN) (see example in Appendix C, "Joint Air Operations Plan Template").

(2) **Recommend to the JFC air apportionment priorities** that should be devoted to the various air operations for a given period of time, after considering objective, priority, or other criteria and consulting with other component commanders.

(3) **Allocate and task** the joint air capabilities and forces made available by the Service components based on the JFC's air apportionment decision.

(4) Provide the JFACC's guidance in the air operations directive (AOD) for the use of joint air capabilities for a specified period that is used throughout the planning stages of the joint air tasking cycle and the execution of the ATO. The AOD may include the JFC's apportionment decision, the JFACC's intent, objectives, weight of effort, and other detailed planning guidance that includes priority of joint air support to JFC and other component operations (see Appendix D, "Air Operations Directive Template").

(5) **Provide oversight and guidance during execution of joint air operations**, to include making timely adjustments to taskings of available joint air forces. The JFACC coordinates with the JFC and affected component commanders, as appropriate, or when the situation requires changes to planned joint air operations.

(6) **Assess the results of joint air operations** and forward assessments to the JFC to support the overall assessment effort.

(7) Perform the duties of the **airspace control authority (ACA),** if designated.

For further detailed discussion of ACA, see JP 3-52, Joint Airspace Control.

(8) Perform the duties of the **area air defense commander (AADC),** if designated.

For more information on AADC, see JP 3-01, Countering Air and Missile Threats.

(9) Perform the duties of the **space coordinating authority (SCA),** if designated. The SCA is responsible for planning, integrating, and coordinating space operations support in the operational area and has primary responsibility for joint space operations planning, to include ascertaining space requirements within the joint force. If the individual designated to be the JFACC is also designated to be the SCA, he/she will normally designate a senior space officer who facilitates coordination, integration, and staffing activities for space operations on a daily basis.

For further detailed discussion of SCA, see JP 3-14, Space Operations.

(10) Perform the duties of the **PR coordinator,** as required.

For further detailed discussion of PR, see JP 3-50, Personnel Recovery.

(11) In concert with the above responsibilities, perform tasks within various mission areas to include, but not limited to:

(a) Defensive counterair (DCA) and offensive counterair (OCA).

(b) CAS.

(c) Airborne ISR and incident awareness and assessment.

(d) Air mobility operations.

(e) Strategic attack.

(f) Air interdiction.

3. Airspace Control Authority

a. The ACA is a commander designated by the JFC to assume overall responsibility for the operation of the airspace control system (ACS) in the airspace control area. Developed by the ACA and approved by the JFC, the ACP establishes general guidance for the control of airspace and procedures for the ACS for the joint force operational area (see Figure II-1). The ACO implements specific control procedures for established time periods. It defines and establishes airspace for military operations as coordinated by the ACA, and notifies all agencies of the effective time of activation and the structure of the airspace. The ACO is normally published either as part of the ATO or as a separate document, and provides the details of the approved requests for airspace coordinating measures (ACMs). All air missions are subject to the ACO and the ACP. The ACO and ACP provide direction to integrate, coordinate, and deconflict the use of airspace within the operational area. (Note: This does not imply any level of command authority over any air assets.) Methods of airspace control vary by military operation and level of conflict from positive control of all air assets in an airspace control area to procedural control of all such assets, or any effective combination (see Figure II-2).

b. **Airspace Control Considerations.** Airspace control is provided to reduce the risk of friendly fire, enhance air defense operations, and permit greater flexibility of operations. The JFC will determine the degree of airspace control required in the joint operations area (JOA). Depending on the mission, ROE, and weapons engagement zones, the degree of control of air assets may need to be rigorous, close, and restrictive, especially in an operational environment that can transition quickly from combat to noncombat and back again.

(1) Airspace control may require a combination of positive control, procedural control, and real-time joint battle management to control the operational activity of the joint force including strict constraints on the forces, weapons, and tactics employed. Additionally,

---

Airspace Control Procedures Objectives

- Enhance effectiveness in accomplishing the joint force commander's objectives.
- Prevent mutual interference.
- Facilitate air defense identification.
- Safely accommodate and expedite the flow of all air traffic in the operational area.
- Prevent friendly fire.
- Facilitate dynamic targeting.

Figure II-1. Airspace Control Procedures Objectives

Methods of Airspace Control

Positive Control

Positively identifies, tracks, and directs air assets using:

- Radars
- Other senses
- Identification, friend or foe
- Selective identification feature
- Digital data links
- Other elements of the communications system

Procedural Control

Relies on previously agreed to and distributed control procedures and measures such as:

- Comprehensive air defense identification procedures and rules of engagement
- Airspace coordinating measures
- Aircraft identification maneuvers
- Fire support coordination measures
- Maneuver control measures

Figure II-2. Methods of Airspace Control

airspace control planning should include contingency operations to account for adversary interference. Such interference may inhibit positive control. In such a scenario, procedural control measures should be used. The JFC may set a coordinating altitude for designated airspace in the JOA. No matter what methods the JFC chooses, they need to be continually evaluated for effectiveness and efficiency as the environment and mission change.

(2) As a matter of controlling joint air operations, the JFC may require **all air missions, including fixed-wing, rotary-wing, tiltrotor, manned and unmanned (except small hand-held systems) of all components, to appear on the appropriate ATO and/or flight plan.** Also, all aircrew and unmanned aircraft (UA) operators must adhere to approved operational procedures. Typically these procedures are promulgated by the JFACC in the SPINS annex of the ATO. The mix of friendly, adversary, and neutral aircraft and mission constraints may require the JFC to strictly control flights in the operational area. In such situations, the JFACC may elect to augment forward theater air-ground system (TAGS) elements with additional planning personnel, training, and capabilities.

c. **ACA Responsibilities.** The ACA achieves airspace control through positive or procedural methods. This includes centralized direction of the ACP, with the authority of the ACOs, supplemented by ACMs, and coupled with an ACS. The ACA should coordinate with joint force components' liaisons prior to commencement of operations. **The ACA must integrate and coordinate the airspace requirements of all the components.** The ACA does not have the authority to approve or disapprove combat operations. That authority is only vested in operational commanders. The ACA assumes responsibility for the ACS in the designated operational area. Subject to the authority and approval of the JFC, the broad responsibilities of the ACA include:

(1) Coordinate and integrate the use of the airspace control area.

---

(2) Develop broad policies and procedures for airspace control and for the coordination required among all users of airspace within the airspace control area.

(3) Establish an ACS that provides for integration of host and other affected nations' constraints and requirements.

(4) Coordinate and deconflict airspace control area user requirements.

(5) Promulgate ACS policies and procedures via the JFC-approved ACP.

d. A key responsibility of the ACA is to provide the flexibility needed within the ACS to meet contingency situations that necessitate rapid employment of forces as well as dynamic changes made by component staffs. The ACO is published either as part of the ATO or as a separate document.

For further detailed discussion of ACA, see JP 3-52, Joint Airspace Control.

4. Area Air Defense Commander

a. **The AADC is responsible for DCA operations, which include the integrated air defense system for the JOA.** DCA and OCA operations combine as the counterair mission, which is designed to attain and maintain the degree of air superiority desired by the JFC. In coordination with the component commanders, the AADC develops, integrates, and distributes a JFC-approved joint AADP. The AADP should be integrated with the ACP to ensure airspace control areas/sectors are synchronized with air defense regions/sectors. Typically, for forces made available for DCA, the AADC retains TACON of air sorties, while surface-based air and missile defense forces (e.g., Patriot missile systems) may be provided in support from another component commander. As such, the US Army Air and Missile Defense Command (AAMDC) should be collocated with the joint air operations center (JAOC), if established, and conduct collaborative counterair intelligence preparation of the battlespace (IPB), planning, and execution control. In distributed operations, the AAMDC may not be in the JAOC but is still functionally tied to it. The Navy component commander (NCC) (or JFMCC, if designated) exercises OPCON of maritime multi-mission and missile defense ships. When designated, these air and missile defense capabilities are in direct support of the AADC for C2 and execution of air defense.

b. **Area Air Defense Considerations. DCA operations** are **integrated with other air operations within the operational area through the AADP** (see sample AADP in JP 3-01, *Countering Air and Missile Threats*). The AADC normally is responsible for developing an integrated air defense system by integrating the capabilities of different components with a robust C2 architecture. **Because of their time-sensitive nature, DCA operations require streamlined coordination and decision-making processes, facilitated by the AADP.** The AADP is the integration of active air defense design, passive defense measures, and the C2 system to provide a comprehensive approach to defending against the threat. It should address command relationships, the adversary and friendly situations, the AADC's intent, CONOPS, and logistics and C2 requirements, as well as detailed weapons control and engagement procedures. Weapons control procedures and airspace control procedures for all air defense weapon systems and forces must be established. These procedures must facilitate

DCA operations while minimizing the risk of friendly fire. Planners must understand they routinely will be required to modify the AADP due to the dynamic nature of joint counterair operations. Ideally, as the JFC's operation/campaign progresses and the AADP is refined, the combination of DCA and OCA operations should diminish the enemy's ability to conduct air and missile attacks, reducing the requirement for DCA operations and the threat to the JFC's freedom of action.

For further detailed discussion, see JP 3-01, Countering Air and Missile Threats.

c. **AADC responsibilities** include planning, integration, synchronization, and coordination of DCA operations with other tactical operations throughout the JOA. This may be facilitated by the JFC's designation of regional and sector air defense commanders. Additional AADC responsibilities include:

(1) Develop, integrate, and distribute a JFC-approved AADP in coordination with Service and functional components.

(2) Develop and execute a detailed plan to disseminate timely air and missile warning and cueing information to components, forces, multinational partners, and civil authorities, as appropriate, in coordination with the intelligence directorate of a joint staff (J-2), the operations directorate of a joint staff (J-3), and the communications system directorate of a joint staff.

(3) Develop and implement identification and engagement procedures that are appropriate to the air and missile threats.

(4) Establish timely and accurate track reporting procedures among participating units to provide a consistent common operational picture.

(5) Establish air defense sectors or regions, as appropriate, to enhance decentralized execution of DCA.

(6) Establish a framework to prevent friendly fire.

(7) Coordinate the protection of those assets listed on the defended asset list (DAL).

d. **Implementation of the AADP** takes place through the AOD, weekly SPINS, and the SPINS annex of the ATO (i.e., daily SPINS).

SECTION B. EXERCISING COMMAND AND CONTROL

5. Joint Air Operations Command and Control System

a. **Joint Air Operations C2 System.** The C2 system for joint air operations will vary depending on the operational area and specific missions. Given the flexibility of modern C2 capabilities, geographic considerations have less of an impact on organizational structure today than in the past. The entire C2 system may be spread across the operational area or concentrated in a specific location, either in close proximity to the fight or far from it. Ultimately, there is no standard template for C2 design.

(1) Normally, the joint air operation C2 system will be built around the C2 system of the Service component commander designated as the JFACC. Each of the Service commanders has an organic system designed for C2 of their air operations. Whether it is the Air Force's theater air control system (TACS), the Army air-ground system (AAGS), the Navy's composite warfare commander (CWC)/Navy tactical air control system (NTACS), Marine air command and control system (MACCS), or the special operations air-ground system (SOAGS) that serves as the nucleus for C2 of joint air operations, the remainder will be integrated to best support the JFC's CONOPS.

(2) **TAGS.** When all elements of the TACS, AAGS, CWC/NTACS, MACCS with fire support coordination center hierarchy, and SOAGS integrate, the entire system is labeled the TAGS. Technology has improved the JFACC's ability to command and control joint air power. The speed of modern warfare, as well as the precision of today's weapons, dictates close coordination in the operational area among the JFC's components. The JFACC ensures that the C2 architecture supports joint air operations by primarily relying upon assigned subordinate C2 elements (e.g., Air Force forces TACS). Other TAGS elements may be made available for tasking to enhance C2 of joint air operations if required. The other components' elements facilitate C2 of their component's operations as an integrated part of the TAGS, and do not receive directions/tasking direct from the JFACC or JAOC unless made available to support/augment the JFACC's ability to command and control joint air operations or accomplish other JFC delegated authorities. TAGS elements roles, responsibilities, and authorities should be clearly spelled out in theater-wide documents such as the AADP, ACP, SPINS, etc., particularly when tasks exceed their component commander's normal scope of operations.

b. **Air Force**

(1) **The TACS is the commander, Air Force forces (COMAFFOR) mechanism** for commanding and controlling component air and space power. It consists of airborne and ground elements to conduct **tailored C2 of air and space operations during military operations,** including air defense, airspace control, and coordination of space mission support not resident within theater. The structure of the TACS should reflect sensor coverage, component liaison elements, and the communications systems required to provide adequate support. As an organic Air Force system, element of the TACS remain under OPCON of the COMAFFOR. In multinational commands, the name and function of certain TACS elements may differ, however, multinational air components have similar capabilities.

(2) **The air operations center (AOC) is the senior C2 element of the TACS** and includes personnel and equipment of necessary disciplines to ensure the effective planning and conduct of component air and space operations (e.g., communications, operations, ISR). The AOC is designed to expand with joint augmentation to form the JAOC when the COMAFFOR is designated by the JFC as the JFACC.

(3) **Air Support Operations Center (ASOC).** The ASOC is the primary control agency of the TACS for execution of air power in direct support of land operations. Its primary mission is to control air operations short of the fire support coordination line or in its assigned area. Normally collocated with the senior Army fires element, the ASOC coordinates and directs air support for land forces. The ASOC is directly subordinate to the AOC, and is responsible for the coordination and control of air component missions in its assigned area.

(a) The tactical air control party (TACP) is an air liaison unit collocated with ground maneuver units. TACPs are OPCON to the ASOC and have two primary missions: advise ground commanders on the capabilities and limitations of air operations and provide the joint terminal attack controllers (JTACs) that perform primary control of CAS attack aircraft. A forward air controller (airborne) is an extension of the TACP and is a specially trained and qualified aviation officer who exercises control of CAS aircraft while airborne.

(b) United States Air Force (USAF) ASOC and TACP personnel at the Army division will normally be integrated with the division fires cell and airspace element to form a joint air-ground integration center (JAGIC). A JAGIC is designed to fully integrate and coordinate fires and air operations over and within the division commander's AO.

(4) Other elements of the TACS include the control and reporting center (CRC) and the airborne warning and control system (AWACS). Both provide battle management, early warning and surveillance, weapons control, and data link management. The CRC is a ground-based mobile radar while AWACS is an airborne radar system. Finally, the joint surveillance target attack radar system is an airborne wide-area surveillance ground moving target indicator and synthetic aperture radar. It provides battle management, early warning and surveillance of ground targets, weapons control, and ISR support.

c. **Army**

(1) **AAGS.** The AAGS is the Army's control system to synchronize, coordinate, and integrate air and ground operations with the ground commander's CONOPS. AAGS provides the framework to initiate and process air support requests (AIRSUPREQs), collection requirements, airspace coordination, joint fires, air and missile defense, and exchange of liaisons. It is used to deconflict airpace users (including air and missile defense and fires) and other warfighting functions with the Army ground commander's scheme of maneuver. The Army depends on its joint partners for capabilities that do not reside within the Army. Other elements such as the TACP, ASOC, and air naval gunfire liaison company belong to different Services. They function as a single entity to plan, coordinate, and integrate air support operations with unified land operations. The Army and Air Force routinely operate in this capacity, and it is referred to as TACS-AAGS (see Figure II-3).

(2) The AAGS provides interface between Army and air support agencies of other Services to plan, evaluate, process, and coordinate air support requirements and operations. Utilizing organic staff members and communications systems, the AAGS works in conjunction with the TACS to coordinate and integrate Air Force and/or joint air support with Army maneuver and fires. Airspace control is also part of the AAGS. The AAGS helps

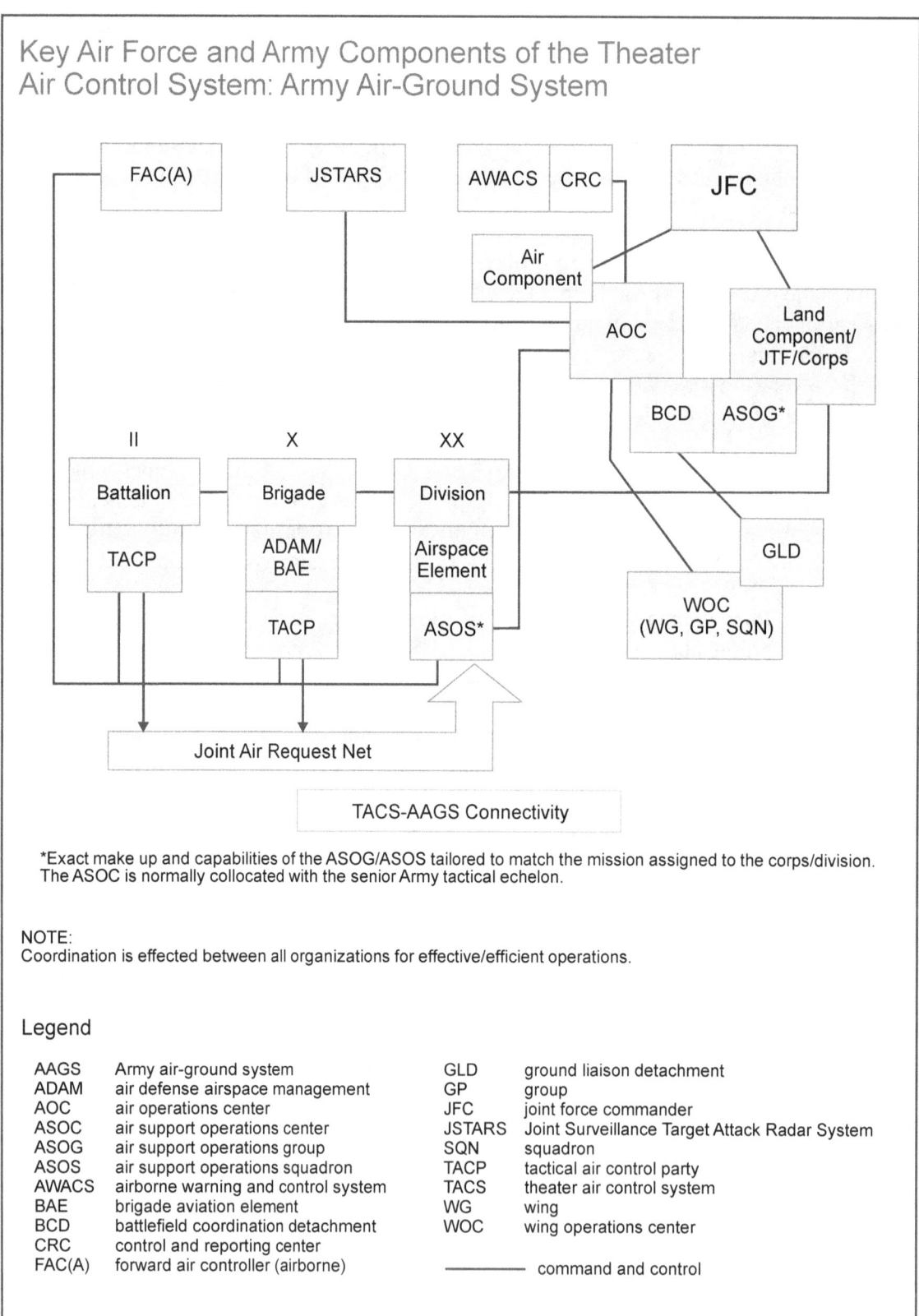

Figure II-3. Key Air Force and Army Components of the Theater Air Control System: Army Air-Ground System

ground commanders and staffs integrate and synchronize Army airspace users with the other airspace users in the operational area. The Army's application of airspace control is to coordinate assigned and supporting airspace user requirements as an integral part of the operations process. Airspace control is an Army commander's responsibility and is part of risk management. Airspace elements are at the senior Army echelon and extend down through all tactical command levels to maneuver units. Corps/division airspace element sections are responsible for airspace control over their entire assigned AO, regardless of whether the AO has been further subdivided into brigade AOs. When a corps/division divides part of its AO to a subordinate brigade some airspace control responsibilities may be delegated. The air defense airspace management (ADAM)/brigade aviation element (BAE) cell is located in the brigade combat team. The ADAM/BAE coordinates airspace requirements with higher headquarters as well as other affected joint forces.

    d. **Navy**

    (1) The **maritime operations center (MOC)** provides the commander (numbered fleet commander, NCC, or JFMCC) with a functionally organized staff and C2 systems, to include collaborative air planning tools such as the theater battle management core system (TBMCS). Operational-level air planning occurs in the MOC. The MOC conducts planning for naval strike, air interdiction, Tomahawk land attack missile operations, naval surface fire support, missile defense, maritime patrol and reconnaissance aircraft operations, and PR missions. Maritime air operations' planning is collaborative involving the MOC, the JAOC, and Navy task force commanders and other subordinate staffs. The JFMCC/NCC will typically establish a naval and amphibious liaison element (NALE) to coordinate with the AOC on matters pertaining to Navy and Marine amphibious, maritime, and air operations, and to serve as the MOC's primary point of contact in the AOC. The NALE director is the JFMCC/NCC's personal representative to the JFACC and will act as the interface between the JFMCC/NCC and the JFACC. The JFMCC/NCC provides overall operational-level guidance and planning. Tactical air planning is conducted largely by subordinate forces at sea.

    (2) CWC doctrine enables the officer in tactical command (OTC) of a naval force to conduct combat operations against air, surface, and subsurface threats while contributing to the overall campaign plan of the JFC. The OTC (typically the JFMCC/NCC in AOs with multiple task forces) may delegate authority to a CWC to conduct some or all of the offensive and defensive functions of the maritime force. Critical air operations positions under the CWC include the strike warfare commander, the air and missile defense commander, ACA, and the air resource element coordinator. The warfare commanders normally exercise TACON over assigned assets. If there are multiple carrier strike groups, expeditionary strike groups, and/or amphibious ready groups operating within a maritime AO, more than one CWC may be designated.

    (3) During amphibious operations, NTACS is the Navy system to control and coordinate all air operations within an amphibious objective area (AOA) or AO. Its counterpart is the MACCS. The NTACS is comprised of the Navy tactical air control center (Navy TACC), tactical air direction center, and helicopter direction center. The Navy TACC is the primary air control agency within the amphibious operations area from which all air operations supporting the amphibious task force are controlled.

e. **Marine Corps**

(1) The MACCS consists of various air C2 agencies designed to provide the Marine air-ground task force (MAGTF) commander the ability to C2 aviation assets in the application of the six functions of Marine aviation: anti-air warfare; offensive air support; assault support; electronic warfare; aerial reconnaissance; and the control of aircraft and missiles.

(2) **Marine Corps Tactical Air Command Center (Marine TACC).** The aviation combat element (ACE) commander exercises air operations authority through the MACCS. The Marine TACC is the senior MACCS agency. It is the operational wing command post from which the ACE commander and his staff plan, supervise, coordinate, and execute MAGTF air operations (this includes the planning and execution of all ATOs and the execution of the current ACE operation order or fragmentary order). It integrates the six functions of Marine aviation with the MAGTF command element through linkage with the MAGTF combat operations center and the force fires coordination center. The Marine TACC provides functional interface for employment of MAGTF aviation in joint and multinational operations. The Marine TACC is similar to the US Air Force AOC. The Marine TACC uses subordinate agencies to facilitate the centralized command and decentralized control of the MAGTF's air assets. These agencies follow:

(a) **Direct Air Support Center (DASC).** The DASC is the MACCS's principal air control agency responsible for the direction of air operations directly supporting ground forces. The DASC processes immediate AIRSUPREQs; coordinates aircraft employment with other supporting arms; manages terminal control assets supporting the ground combat element (GCE) and logistics combat element forces; and controls assigned aircraft, unmanned aircraft systems (UASs), and itinerant aircraft transiting through DASC controlled airspace. The DASC controls and directs air support activities that affect the GCE commander's focus on close operations and those air missions requiring integration with the ground combat forces (CAS, assault support, and designated air reconnaissance). It is similar to the US Air Force ASOC.

(b) **Tactical Air Operations Center (TAOC).** The TAOC performs three primary functions within the MACCS: air surveillance, air direction, and air control. As the MAGTF's primary air surveillance agency, the TAOC uses its organic radars and tactical data links to create a recognized air picture within its assigned sector. The air picture, which is shared through various data links to a wide variety of C2 systems, is managed through detailed coordination with higher and adjacent MAGTF and joint surveillance platforms. The TAOC also performs positive and procedural air control under a variety of delegated air direction functions, including coordination and deconfliction of airspace, anti-air warfare, tanker management, asset management, routing of itinerant aircraft, and coordination and control of fires in the deep area of the battlespace. The TAOC is similar to the US Air Force CRC.

(c) **Marine Air Traffic Control (ATC).** The Marine ATC provides all weather radar and non-radar approach, departure, en route, and tower ATC services to friendly aircraft. It is the principal terminal ATC organization with the MACCS and serves as the ATC interface with other military C2 agencies and civilian agencies to include the Federal Aviation Administration (FAA) and the International Civil Aviation Organization. It is designed to work within the MACCS structure but can work independently as part of a joint force should the mission dictate. Marine ATC also serves as an integral part of the MAGTF integrated air defense system providing the air picture for base defense zones of operation around associated airfields.

f. Special Operations

(1) Theater special operations are normally under the control of the commander, theater special operations command (TSOC). The commander of a TSOC may also function as the joint force special operations component commander (JFSOCC) for a joint force. The commander of a TSOC or the JFSOCC may designate a joint special operations air component commander (JSOACC) to control SOF aviation. The JSOACC is normally for planning and executing joint special operations air activities. If a JSOACC is not designated then SOF aviation is normally controlled by a Service component within the joint force special operations command. The SOAGS serves as the nucleus for C2 of special operations air activities. Principal organizations and personnel that support the SOAGS are the JSOACC, special operations liaison element (SOLE), special tactics teams, and terminal attack control special operations personnel. Whether operating autonomously or in conjunction with conventional forces, special operations must be synchronized and closely coordinated with other air operations conducted in theater. In order to coordinate and deconflict operations, the JFSOCC and the JFACC exchange liaison teams.

(2) The SOLE is a team provided by the JFSOCC that is attached to the JFACC or appropriate Service component air C2 organization to coordinate, deconflict, and synchronize special operations air and surface operations with conventional air operations. The SOLE director works directly for the JFSOCC as a liaison and has no command authority for mission tasking, planning, and execution. The SOLE provides coordination for the visibility of SOF operations in the ATO and the ACO. The SOLE must also coordinate appropriate fire support coordination measures between the JAOC and the SOF HQ to help prevent friendly fire.

For more information on the SOLE, see JP 3-05, Special Operations.

6. Joint Force Air Component Command Organization

a. JFACC

(1) The JFACC should establish a close working relationship with the JFC to ensure the optimum employment of joint air power. This working relationship should extend through the JFC and JFACC staffs, as well as the other component staffs that play a crucial role in supporting the JFC with air power capabilities. **The JFACC will normally operate from a JAOC.** The JAOC and the JFACC's staff should be manned with subject matter experts who reflect the capabilities/forces available to the JFACC for tasking and include appropriate component representation. This representation will provide the JFACC with the knowledge and experience required. JFACC staff billets requiring specific expertise or

individuals should be identified, staffed accordingly, trained, and employed during peacetime exercises to ensure their preparedness for military operations. To be most effective, the JFACC should incorporate appropriate component representation throughout the JAOC and staff, rather than just limiting them to liaison positions.

Note: The JAOC staff is under the command of the JFACC. This staff should not be confused with organizational liaisons that remain under the command of their parent organization. See paragraph 8, "Liaisons," for more on liaisons to the JAOC.

(2) **JAOC Organization. The JAOC is structured to operate as a fully integrated command center and should be staffed by members of all participating components, to include key staff positions, in order to fulfill the JFACC's responsibilities.** A JAOC provides the capability to plan, coordinate, allocate, task, execute, monitor, and assess the activities of assigned or attached forces. Through the JAOC, the JFACC monitors execution of joint air operations and directs changes as the situation dictates. As a synchronizing C2 mechanism of the TAGS and focal point for ATO execution, the JAOC should have secure and redundant communications with operations, logistics, weather, and intelligence centers, higher and lateral headquarters, as well as subordinate units to preclude degradation in its ability to control joint air forces. **JAOC organizations may differ. Elements that should be common to all JAOCs are the strategy division (SD), combat plans division (CPD), intelligence, surveillance, and reconnaissance division (ISRD), air mobility division (AMD), and combat operations division (COD).** Divisions, cells, or teams within the JAOC should be established as needed (see Appendix E, "Joint Air Operations Center Divisions and Descriptions," for JAOC divisions and descriptions). The JAOC director is responsible to the JFACC for integrating the planning, coordinating, allocating, tasking, executing, and assessing tasks for all joint air operations, and coordinates with the director of mobility forces (DIRMOBFOR) to meet airlift and tanker priorities with support of United States Transportation Command (USTRANSCOM) mobility forces. Planning future joint air operations and assessing the effectiveness of past operations is usually the responsibility of the SD, while the CPD is usually devoted to near-term planning and drafting of the daily ATO. Execution of the daily ATO is carried out by the COD and closely follows the action of current joint operations, shifting air missions from their scheduled times or targets, and making other adjustments as the situation requires. The AMD is normally responsible for integrating intertheater and intratheater airlift, aerial refueling, and aeromedical evacuation (AE) into air plans and tasking orders, and for coordinating with the JFC movement requirements and control authority and Air Mobility Command's Tanker Airlift Control Center. The ISRD provides the JFACC with predictive and actionable intelligence, targeting support, and collection management expertise to support the air tasking cycle. Each of the JAOC's major activities relies on expertise from **liaisons** (e.g., battlefield coordination detachment [BCD], AAMDC liaison team, NALE, Air Force liaison element [AFLE], SOLE, Marine liaison element [MARLE]) to coordinate requests or requirements and maintain a current and relevant picture of the other component operations. For more on liaisons, see Appendix F, "Liaison Elements within the Joint Air Operations Center."

For further detail on air mobility, see Chapter III, "Planning and Execution of Joint Air Operations," paragraph 8, "Air Mobility Considerations," and JP 3-17, Air Mobility Operations.

(a) **Functional Area and Mission Experts.** Functional area experts (such as force protection, intelligence, meteorological and oceanographic, logistics, space operations, legal, airspace, plans, and communications personnel) provide the critical expertise in support, plans, execution, and assessment functions. Mission experts in air-to-air, air-to-ground, ground-to-air, information operations (IO), intelligence, air refueling, PR, and other areas provide the technical warfighting expertise required to plan for joint air operations and employ capabilities/forces made available by the components. Functional and mission experts from all components will provide manning throughout the JAOC and at all levels of command, and may be organized in special teams. Reachback capability (such as the United States Strategic Command (USSTRATCOM) Center for Combating Weapons of Mass Destruction (WMD) and the Defense Threat Reduction Agency) can be used for technical issues related to planning, targeting, collateral damage estimates, joint intelligence preparation of the operational environment (JIPOE), and force protection.

(b) **Preparation. The nucleus of the JFACC's staff should be formally educated and trained to perform fundamental operational activities in joint air operations and be representative of the joint force.** Staff augmentation with manning as identified above ensures joint representation throughout the JAOC. The JFACC, in coordination with other component commanders, will determine specific manning requirements based on the size and scope of the operation, force list, and personnel availability.

(c) Finally, **the role of intelligence is extremely important** and is an integral part of the daily functions of the JAOC. Intelligence personnel monitor and assess adversary capabilities and intentions, especially WMD threats, and provide assistance in target, weapon, fuse, and platform selection, including UA recommendations, and WMD response. In coordination with the SD's operational assessment team, they also conduct an assessment of the effectiveness of combat operations and provide an up-to-date picture of the adversary, expected adversary operations, and the status and priority of assigned targets to assist in execution day changes.

(3) The JFACC may establish one or more joint air component coordination elements (JACCEs) with other commanders' headquarters to better integrate joint air operations with their operations. When established, the JACCE is a component-level liaison that serves as the direct representative of the JFACC. The JACCE does not perform any C2 functions and the JACCE director does not have command authority over any air forces. The JACCE is established by the JFACC to better integrate with other component's senior deployed headquarters. JACCE may also be assigned to the supported JTF headquarters (if the theater JFACC is designated in support to a JTF) to better integrate air component operations within the overall joint force. When established, the JACCE acts as the JFACC's primary representative to the respective commander and facilitates interaction among the respective staff to communicate, advise, coordinate, and support effective interplay. JACCE expertise should include plans, operations, ISR, space, airspace management, air mobility, and administrative and communications support.

See Appendix G, "The Joint Air Component Coordination Element," for JACCE responsibilities and notional organization.

(4) **Tasking Component Forces**

(a) The JFC directs and controls the joint air effort by providing broad guidance, prioritized objectives, targeting priorities, procedures, and assigning appropriate authorities to subordinate commanders. Each component commander may be tasked to support other components and/or to provide support to the joint force as a whole. The JFACC, in consultation with other component commanders, is responsible for the air apportionment recommendation to the JFC, who makes the air apportionment decision.

(b) Forces are tasked by the JFACC based on the JFC's approval of the JFACC's air apportionment recommendation (e.g., CAS, interdiction). In the case of a theater JFACC, the GCC will decide what air capabilities/forces are provided to each subordinate JFC. The air apportionment decision referenced here is made by each subordinate JFC.

(c) Component forces must comply with the ROE, ACP, ACO, AADP, and SPINS. The ATO includes all known and prospective aircraft (alert, medical evacuation, PR, etc.) that may fly during that ATO day, even if not apportioned to the JFACC. The overarching intent is to identify all potential flights to airspace managers and users in the JOA. Some smaller (Group 1) UASs may not be included on the ATO based on use and mission requirements. The inclusion of air assets in the ATO does not imply any change in command relationships or tasking authority over them, nor does it restrict component commanders' flexibility to respond to the dynamics of the operational environment.

For more information on UAS groups, see Chapter III, "Planning and Execution of Joint Air Operations," paragraph 9, "Unmanned Aircraft Systems Considerations."

(d) **Army forces (ARFOR) conduct land operations in an assigned AO.** The Army identifies air support requirements to the supporting air component or JFACC. Likewise the JFACC may require mutual support and ARFOR may be made available to the JFACC in a support relationship. The integration of Army assets/forces, to include UASs, aviation and fires, with the air component's operations requires detailed planning and coordination.

(e) **Marine Corps Aviation Assets.** The MAGTF commander will retain OPCON of organic air assets. The primary mission of the MAGTF ACE is to support the MAGTF GCE. During joint operations, the MAGTF aviation assets will normally be in support of the MAGTF mission. The MAGTF commander will make sorties available to the JFC for tasking through the JFACC, for air defense, long-range air interdiction, and long-range reconnaissance. Sorties in excess of MAGTF direct support requirements will be provided to the JFC for tasking through the JFACC for the support of other components of the joint force or the joint force as a whole.

NOTE: Sorties provided for air defense, long-range interdiction, and long-range reconnaissance are not "excess" sorties and will be covered in the ATO. These sorties provide a distinct contribution to the overall joint force effort. The JFC must exercise integrated control of air defense, long-range reconnaissance, and long-range interdiction aspects of the joint operation or theater campaign, and these sorties provide a distinct contribution to the joint force effort.

(f) **Navy Aviation Assets.** Navy assets normally are retained for employment in support of the assigned joint maritime missions, including sea control, deterrence, and maritime power projection within the operational area. Assets include sea- and land-based naval aircraft. Navy assets not required for assigned joint missions or for fleet defense will normally be made available for tasking via the joint air tasking process.

(g) **Air Force Air and Space Assets.** The air expeditionary task force (AETF) is the primary means by which the Air Force presents forces to a JFC during contingency operations. AETFs are sized and tailored to meet the JFC's specific mission requirements. Air Force assets include bombers, specialized reconnaissance, C2 air and ground platforms and centers, air mobility aircraft, single and multi-role fighters, and UASs. Air Force capabilities also include intertheater and intratheater airlift; air-to-air refueling; ISR; PR/combat search and rescue; and extensive space assets. To plan, execute, and assess air and space operations, the Air Force has developed tailored Air Force AOCs to exercise C2 of the full range of Air Force air, space, and cyberspace capabilities for a joint force. These AOCs may be further tailored to address changing operational environments, and may be augmented by operations centers anywhere else in the world. With the exception of certain national assets, special operations, and intertheater air mobility assets, the COMAFFOR will normally have OPCON over Air Force assets in the operational area. In most cases, Air Force assigned or attached aircraft are made available for employment as directed by the JFACC.

(h) **SOF Assets.** SOF aviation assets are normally retained as an integral part of the joint special operations mission. Theater SOF aviation assets are typically only sufficient to support special operations mission requirements. Assets and aircrews not represented on the daily ATO are routinely planning or being prepared for subsequent special operations. Excess sorties may be made available for JFC tasking in support of other operations. When SOF aviation assets are employed primarily in support of conventional air operations, the JFC may make these sorties available to the JFACC for tasking. Command relationships, launch authority, and other coordination measures between the components should specifically address situations where the same SOF aviation assets may be tasked to conduct missions for both components during the same ATO period. JFACC coordination is normally accomplished through the SOLE located in the JAOC. The JACCE coordinates with the SOF organization, representing the JFACC's needs in either a supporting or supported role.

(5) **Options for Establishing a Joint Force Air Component Command. Options available to a GCC during contingency operations to establish a joint force air component command include: designating a sub-theater (e.g., subunified or JTF) JFACC; a theater JFACC operating in support of subunified or JTF-level commands; or a combination of a theater and sub-theater JFACCs.**

(a) **Designated JFACC for Sub-Theater Commands.** When a GCC establishes a subordinate JTF to conduct operations and air forces are attached, with specification of OPCON to the subordinate JFC, the JFC has the option of designating a JFACC. This option will place dedicated air assets and independent C2 capability under the OPCON of the JFC for whom they are performing the mission. It provides unity of command over the forces employed within the assigned JOA and greater direct control and predictability as to which air assets are available. When there is only one JTF in a given theater, this is normally the preferred option.

(b) **Theater JFACC.** When a GCC establishes multiple JTFs within the area of responsibility (AOR), the GCC normally will retain C2 of joint air forces at the GCC level. Joint air forces will be controlled to support the multiple JTF commanders according to the JTF commanders' objectives and the GCC's AOR-wide priorities. In this situation, joint air forces are controlled at the theater level, under the direction of the "theater JFACC," subordinate to the GCC. The theater-level JFACC provides flexibility in managing limited air assets to meet the requirements of the GCC and multiple JTFs. When there are multiple JTFs in one GCC's AOR, this is normally the preferred option.

1. The theater JFACC will be the supporting commander to the GCC's subordinate JTF commanders' joint air operations within their respective JOAs. Per JP 1, *Doctrine for the Armed Forces of the United States,* an establishing directive should be promulgated to clearly delineate support command relationships. Unless limited by the establishing directive, the supported JTF commanders will have the authority to exercise general direction of the supporting effort. (General direction includes the designation and prioritization of targets or objectives, timing and duration of the supporting action, and other instructions necessary for coordination and efficiency.)

2. The theater JFACC, as the supporting commander, determines the forces, tactics, methods, procedures, and communications to be employed in providing this support. The JFACC will advise and coordinate with the supported JTF commanders on matters concerning the employment and limitations (e.g., logistics) of such support, assist in planning for the integration of such support into the supported JTF commanders' efforts as a whole, and ensure that support requirements are appropriately communicated within the JFACC's organization. When the JFACC cannot fulfill the needs of the supported JTF commander, the GCC will be notified by either the supported JTF commander or JFACC. The GCC is responsible for determining a solution. For their operations, these JTF commanders—as JFCs—will exercise approval authority for products normally generated for "JFC approval" (including products generated by the theater JFACC for their JOA).

3. The theater JFACC may deploy one or more JACCEs to the JTF headquarters and other component headquarters as needed to ensure they receive the appropriate level of joint air support (see Appendix G, "The Joint Air Component Coordination Element," for a more detailed description of JACCE). The JACCE will provide on-hand air expertise to the JTF commanders and the direct link back to the theater JFACC and the JAOC.

(c) **Combination Theater and Sub-Theater Level JFACCs.** There may be a theater and sub-theater level JFACC. While in some cases, this may be the most operationally desirable option, it is also the most demanding on available C2 resources (manpower and equipment).

(d) Between these three options presented there can be other potential organizational variations. While it is impossible to assemble a complete list of all potential C2 arrangements, two additional options that commanders may consider follow:

<u>1.</u> **Multiple JFACCs Sharing a Theater JAOC.** Typical arrangements of this nature have been driven by unforeseen, short-term incidents outside the scope of the original JAOC establishment. In this case, sufficient manning and infrastructure must be in place to support each of the individual JFACC missions prior to establishing such an arrangement. Prioritization and apportionment of limited air and C2 assets must be clearly detailed by the appropriate authority.

<u>2.</u> **Theater JFACC or JTF's JFACC to operate concurrently with a JSOACC** assigned to a commander, joint special operations task force (CDRJSOTF). This is a possible arrangement, although not commonly used, when a joint special operations task force (JSOTF) is formed and air assets not being used at a given time by the CDRJSOTF may be made available to the JFACC for tasking.

b. The options discussed above contain combatant commander (CCDR)/subordinate relationships. Approval authority is inherent in command; therefore, it is imperative that subordinate JFCs exercise approval authority over those processes affecting operations within their JOAs regardless as to whether the products are developed by resources allocated

---

COMMAND AND CONTROL OF AIR OPERATIONS DURING OPERATION ODYSSEY DAWN

On 3 March, 2011, USAFRICOM [United States Africa Command] was directed to establish a JTF [joint task force] under the command of Admiral Samuel Locklear, USN [United States Navy], Commander US Naval Forces Africa, initially to facilitate a noncombatant evacuation operation, provide humanitarian assistance as required, and transport Egyptian civilians from Tunisia to Egypt in support of the US Department of State. This mission soon expanded to include enforcement of maritime exclusion and no-fly zones, and offensive operations to protect the Libyan civilian population. JTF Odyssey Dawn included naval assets from the US 6th Fleet and air assets from both USAFE [United States Air Forces in Europe] and 17 AF [Air Force] (AFAFRICA).

USAFE and 17 AF (AFAFRICA) headquarters were both located at Ramstein Air Base, Germany. As the AF component to USAFRICOM, the 17 AF (AFAFRICA) commander was designated the JFACC [joint force air component commander] supported by 17 AF's 617th AOC [Air Operations Center]. However, 17 AF (AFAFRICA) was organized and resourced primarily for logistics and lift operations, not combat operations. The JFACC received heavy augmentation from the more broadly staffed USAFE and 3 AF's 603rd AOC facility. For Operation Odyssey Dawn, these two staffs in effect merged under the leadership of the 17 AF (AFAFRICA) commander operating out of the 603rd AOC, providing increased capacity for the JFACC.

Libya: Operation ODYSSEY DAWN (OOD)
A Case Study In Command And Control
Joint and Coalition Operational Analysis
4 October 2011

---

to the command or by other headquarters. This includes, but is not limited to: air apportionment decision, targeting products, joint air estimates, JAOP, AOD, ATO, ACP, ACO, and AADP.

7. Joint Force Staff Option

In operations of limited scope, duration, or complexity, or in which air operations are a relatively small aspect of the overall joint force, the JFC may plan, direct, and control joint air operations with the assistance of the JFC staff. In this situation, the JFC would retain command authority and responsibility and would normally request augmentation from appropriate components to perform the C2 air function and assist in planning and coordinating joint air operations. In the joint force staff option all previously discussed JFACC responsibilities will be accomplished by the joint force staff as directed by the JFC.

a. The JFC staff operates out of the joint operations center (JOC). Under the JFC staff option, the JOC also functions as the C2 node for joint air operations. The composition of a joint staff should reflect the composition of the subordinate joint forces to ensure those responsible for employing forces have a thorough knowledge of their capabilities and limitations. The presence of liaisons on a single-Service staff does not transform that Service staff into a joint staff. The joint staff should be composed of appropriate members in key positions of responsibility from each Service or functional component having significant forces assigned to the command. The same general guidelines for joint staffs apply to multinational operations. Key staff positions ought to be a representative mix of US and multinational officers with shared responsibilities and trust.

b. **JFC Staff Authority and Responsibilities.** The JFC staff derives its authority from the JFC. JFC staff relationships and responsibilities must be specified early in the planning process. Although command authority for tasking subordinate commanders is retained by the JFC, the JFC may assign responsibility for coordinating joint air operations to a staff directorate (e.g., J-3), a specific staff officer (e.g., J-3 air officer), or a special staff.

(1) **Planning.** The JFC staff prepares the JAOP to support the JFC's objectives. They may also prepare the ACP, AADPs, and DAL.

(2) **Coordination.** The JFC staff coordinates joint air activities with other operations in the operational area. As appropriate, subordinate commanders and coordinating agencies furnish liaison elements and augmentation personnel to the JFC staff to coordinate with the joint force.

(3) **Execution.** The JFC staff monitors the execution of joint air operations by subordinate commanders tasked through the ATO. This may include redirecting sorties, as directed by the JFC, to accomplish joint force objectives.

(4) **Supporting Operations.** Joint air operations may require support (e.g., suppression of enemy air defenses, ground-based air defense) from resources other than aircraft. The JFC may direct components to support joint air operations with assets, capabilities, or forces, in addition to the air capabilities/forces provided.

8. Liaisons

a. In addition to the JFC and staff, other component commanders and their staffs require continuous and ready access to the JFACC and the JFACC's staff. Principal means of accomplishing this are through personal contact, the established communications and information support system, and liaison personnel. These **liaisons work for their respective component commanders and work with the JFACC and staff.** Each component normally provides liaison elements (BCD, SOLE, NALE, MARLE, AFLE, AAMDC, and others, as appropriate) that work within the JAOC. These liaison elements consist of personnel who provide component planning and tasking expertise and coordination capabilities. They help integrate and coordinate their component's operations with joint air operations. If the JFC retains the functions normally given to a JFACC, then the liaisons would work directly with the JFC's staff responsible for joint air operations.

See Appendix F, "Liaison Elements within the Joint Air Operations Center."

b. **Component Liaisons.** Component liaisons serve as conduits for coordination between the JFACC and their respective component commanders. Functional or Service component commanders should delegate appropriate authority to their liaisons to effectively participate in the JAOC environment and processes. Component commanders should determine liaison responsibilities and authorize direct coordination with specified commanders and staff. They must be equipped and authorized to communicate directly with their respective component commander. The liaisons have the responsibility of presenting component perspectives and considerations regarding planning and executing joint air operations. Component liaisons must be familiar with the details of all component air, surface, and subsurface missions to coordinate their impact on joint air operations and its impact upon them.

c. **Other Liaisons.** Other USG departments and agencies, IGOs, and NGOs conduct activities near or in areas of military operations. CCDRs must be cognizant of these organizations and their actions. To the extent possible, commanders should ensure that these organizations' efforts and military efforts are coordinated and complementary (or at least not in conflict). Commanders should consider establishing coordination and mutual support mechanisms, as needed, to eliminate or mitigate conflict and support US goals in the region. Liaisons from these organizations to the JFACC may be appropriate. Multinational partners, particularly in operations being conducted in conjunction with or in close proximity to those of allied nations, may provide liaisons that work with the JFACC to ease coordination between forces. They work with the JFACC to coordinate the activities of their sending organizations. In addition, the JFACC should consider sending liaisons to appropriate organizations, for example, multinational force intelligence collection, air defense, homeland defense (HD), and airborne related functions.

9. Joint Force Air Component Commander Basing and Transition

Procedures for joint air operations are designed to exploit the flexibility of air power to achieve joint force objectives while providing support to component operations. Joint air operations scenarios may vary, and each scenario requires extensive planning when transition of JFACC responsibilities is necessary. Basing of the JFACC depends on the nature and scale of the operation, and may shift when shifting to a different phase.

a. **Land-Based JFACC.** In large-scale air operations, land-based JFACCs and JAOCs are normally desired because of the enhanced logistics and communications provided by additional equipment and workspaces that may not be available on sea-based facilities.

b. **Sea-Based JFACC.** The JFACC and JAOC may be sea-based when any one of the following conditions are present:

(1) Maritime forces provide the preponderance of air assets and have the organizational construct, operating experience, and management functions capability to effectively plan, task, and control joint air operations.

(2) Land-based facilities or sufficient infrastructure does not exist.

(3) A secure land-based area is not available, and ground support forces are forced to withdraw.

c. **JFACC Transition.** Effective joint air operations planning must contain provisions to transition JFACC responsibilities between components of the joint force and/or JFC's staff. The JFACC transition should be identified in the JAOP.

(1) **Planned Transition.** The JFACC should develop a plan for transition of JFACC duties to another component or location. Planned JFACC transitions are possible as a **function of buildup or scale down of joint force operations.** During transition of JFACC responsibilities, the component passing responsibilities should continue monitoring joint air planning, tasking, and control systems, and remain ready to reassume JFACC responsibilities until the gaining component has achieved full operational capability.

(2) **Unplanned Transition.** During unplanned shifts of JFACC responsibility, as a possible result of battle damage or major C2 equipment failure, a smooth transition is unlikely. Therefore, **the JFC should predesignate alternates** (both inter- and intracomponent) and establish preplanned responses/options to the temporary or permanent loss of primary JFACC capability. Frequent backup and exchange of databases is essential to facilitate a rapid resumption of operations should an unplanned transition occur.

(3) **Transition Events.** The following events may cause the JFACC responsibilities to shift:

(a) Establishment of a subordinate JTF with delegated joint air operations responsibilities and attachment of forces to that JTF.

(b) Coordination requirements, related to ATO planning and execution, exceed the component capability.

(c) Buildup or relocation of forces shifts preponderance of the air capabilities/forces and the ability to effectively plan, task, and control joint air operations to another component commander; and the JFC decides that the other component is in a better position (location, C2 capability, or other considerations) to accomplish the JFACC responsibilities.

(d) C2 systems become unresponsive or unreliable.

(4) **Considerations.** Considerations to aid in JFACC transition planning and decisions include:

(a) Continuous, uninterrupted, and unambiguous guidance and direction for joint air operations must be the primary objective of any JFACC transition.

(b) Appropriate communications system capabilities to ensure shift of JFACC duties is as transparent to the components as possible.

(c) Specific procedures for coordinating and executing planned and unplanned shifts of JFACC should be published in the JAOP.

(d) The relieving component must have adequate communications, connectivity, manning, intelligence support, and C2 capability prior to assuming JFACC responsibilities.

(e) There must be continuous planning to support both the expansion and transition of the communications system to support the JFC's CONOPS for future operations.

(f) The ability to plan, publish, and disseminate an ATO and SPINS.

(g) The JFC's objectives to conduct supporting joint air operations.

(h) Established timely, reliable, and secure communications links with all appropriate coordination cells to facilitate continuous and dynamic exchange of information.

(i) Complete familiarity with the AADP and ACPs.

(j) Complete and current databases to expedite the transition.

d. **Transition of C2 for Joint Air Operations.** The JFC may choose to assign C2 of joint air operations to a JFACC when the duration and scope of joint air operations exceed the JFC's span of control. Additionally, the JFC may transfer designated mission experts and functional area augmentees from the JFC staff to the JFACC's JAOC to assist in the transition and coordination of joint air operations. Conversely, a transition from JFACC to JFC staff may also be directed when the JFC determines that operational requirements warrant such a change.

10. **Communications System**

a. **The JFACC is responsible for identifying and validating joint air requirements that affect the JFC's mission and allow accomplishment of the JFC's directives.**

b. The ability to exchange information via reliable secure communications with the JFC, joint force staff, and other component commanders is key to the successful integration of the joint air effort. Planning should address the following areas:

(1) **Data exchange requirements** should be promulgated as early as possible to ensure that each component can meet interoperable interface requirements. Every effort should be made to confirm data exchange connectivity requirements during planning.

(2) Planning for all information exchange requirements and procedures **should consider all elements of Department of Defense (DOD) information network operations.**

(3) **The best mix of computer-aided systems should be available for data transmission.** The JAOC and liaison elements depend on secure, reliable, beyond-line-of-sight communications and data exchange equipment in order to respond to joint force requirements. For example, the TBMCS is often used. The use of ATO generation and dissemination software portions of TBMCS has been standardized. This ATO feature allows the JAOC to be interoperable with other force-level Service systems.

(4) Centralized control and decentralized execution requires a robust data communications architecture. **Planning should anticipate the need for communications in degraded environments at all levels and phases of operations,** and include considerations for alternate routing, redundant systems, use of other systems, protocols, and message standards. Impaired/inadequate information exchange capability must be anticipated and incorporated into risk management considerations during air operations planning.

For additional information on communication systems, see JP 6-0, Joint Communications System.

11. Command and Control of Joint Air Operations for Defense Support of Civil Authorities and Homeland Defense

a. Commander, United States Northern Command (USNORTHCOM) and Commander, United States Pacific Command (USPACOM) share the primary mission for US HD and defense support of civil authorities (DSCA) within their assigned AORs. For US-only HD and DSCA air operations within continental United States, the 1st Air Force Commander is designated the JFACC. To facilitate operations in Alaska, USNORTHCOM has established JTF-Alaska. The Commander, Pacific Air Forces is the JFACC for the USPACOM AOR. USNORTHCOM is assisted by North American Aerospace Defense Command (NORAD), the bi-national command (US and Canada) that conducts aerospace warning, control, and maritime warning in defense of North America. NORAD is divided into three regions: Continental NORAD Region, Alaskan NORAD Region, and Canadian NORAD Region. Each region has a commander triple-hatted as JFACC, airspace coordination authority, and AADC for executing DCA missions.

b. C2 of joint air operations during routine HD and most DSCA noncrisis operations is conducted under peacetime rules. As with the international community, when no combat operations have been declared, a civil organization is usually the ACA. For the US, this agency is the FAA and for Canada it is NAV CANADA. These agencies are charged by their respective nations with managing airspace, and may request the assistance of their military or NORAD to support airspace control. Operation NOBLE EAGLE is the ongoing operation covering aerospace warning and control for the US and its territories.

c. During DSCA operations, at the request of the lead federal agency and with approval of the Secretary of Defense, the appropriate JFACC, working in support of the FAA, assists in developing procedural control rules for safe use of the airspace by the multitude of participating agencies. Joint forces will coordinate all DSCA air operations with the JFACC to facilitate unity of effort, even while other air activities may be occurring elsewhere in the nation. The USNORTHCOM's JAOC typically establishes and activates an unclassified and voluntary scheduling system to prevent overtaxing fragile or limited control systems. USG departments and agencies can then identify their necessary flight operations to enable collaborative deconfliction.

(1) The Department of Homeland Security (DHS) has overall responsibility for US homeland security (HS), and the DOD may be asked to provide support to DHS for HS operations. DHS has the largest civilian government air force in the world and has peacetime oversight of the United States Coast Guard (USCG). In HS operations it is possible for the JFACC to have the preponderance of military air assets, but not the preponderance of USG air assets to coordinate. During HS operations with a threat emanating from United States Southern Command's (USSOUTHCOM's) AOR, DOD may direct USSOUTHCOM to lead DOD support to DHS, with the USAF Southern Command commander designated as the JFACC.

(2) Although numerous interagency partners are responsible for DSCA mission accomplishment, most air operations fall under the FAA or are impacted by FAA authority. For instance, aerial search and rescue may be accomplished by state (e.g., Army National Guard, Air National Guard, or state police helicopters), federal (e.g., USAF or USCG), or civil (e.g., Civil Air Patrol) agencies, but all still operate within the procedures established by the FAA.

(3) DSCA support is often provided by National Guard forces, either federalized under Title 10, United States Code (USC), Title 32, USC, or state active duty status. Each state, territory, and the District of Columbia has the latitude to develop aviation C2 procedures pursuant to the appropriate governor's directives. Often, these C2 architectures will incorporate many joint concepts. To enhance unity of effort during emergencies, USNORTHCOM's JAOC has pre-coordinated airspace C2 procedures with both the FAA and through the National Guard Bureau as the channel of communications with the numerous state adjutants general. During DSCA operations, the state governors typically retain C2 of civil and National Guard air assets, and execute operations through National Guard joint force headquarters-state or the state's emergency operations center.

d. As the nation moves from peacetime to hostilities, the FAA, NAV CANADA, USNORTHCOM, NORAD, and USPACOM coordinate to provide military support to the civil airspace control agencies. The FAA provides liaisons to USNORTHCOM and USPACOM to collaborate and minimize conflicts during mission execution. In the event the FAA is unable to perform airspace control responsibilities, the appropriate JFACC should be prepared to take over the airspace control role. This may occur at pre-coordinated points, where air defense and some airspace control is accomplished by the military agencies on behalf of the government through the application of emergency security control of air traffic and the declaration of various air defense emergencies. Close cooperation and coordination with interagency partners, including FAA and DHS, is essential.

For additional detailed information on DSCA, see JP 3-28, Defense Support of Civil Authorities. *For additional detailed information on HD, see JP 3-27,* Homeland Defense.

CHAPTER III
PLANNING AND EXECUTION OF JOINT AIR OPERATIONS

> *"It is improbable that any terrorization of the civil population which could be achieved by air attack would compel the government of a great nation to surrender. In our own case, we have seen the combative spirit of the people roused, and not quelled, by the German air raids. Therefore, our air offensive should consistently be directed at striking the bases and communications upon whose structure the fighting power of his armies and fleets of the sea and air depends."*
>
> **Winston Churchill (1917)**

SECTION A. PLANNING AND EXECUTION OF JOINT AIR OPERATIONS

1. Joint Air Operations Planning

While the discussion in this chapter assumes that the JFC has designated a JFACC, if the JFC retained control of joint air operations, the JFC's designated staff would be responsible for the planning and execution of joint air operations and should follow a similar process. Planning for joint air operations begins with **understanding the JFC's mission and intent.** The JFC's **estimate** of the operational environment and articulation of the objectives needed to accomplish the mission form the basis for determining components' objectives. The JFACC uses the JFC's mission, commander's estimate and objectives, commander's intent, CONOPS, and the components' objectives to develop a course of action (COA). When the JFC approves the JFACC's COA, it becomes the basis for more detailed joint air operations planning—expressing what, where, and how joint air operations will affect the adversary or current situation. The JFACC's daily guidance ensures that joint air operations effectively support the joint force objectives while retaining enough flexibility in execution to adjust to the dynamics of military operations (see Figure III-1).

2. The Joint Air Estimate

The joint air estimate is described as a process of reasoning by which the air component commander considers all the circumstances affecting the military situation and decides on a COA to be taken to accomplish the mission. The joint air estimate is often produced as the culmination of the COA development and selection stages of the joint operation planning process. The joint air estimate reflects the JFACC's analysis of the various COAs that may be used to accomplish the assigned mission(s) and contains the recommendation for the best COA. Figure III-2 shows a joint air estimate overview format.

See Appendix B, "Joint Air Estimate of the Situation Template," for more information.

3. The Joint Operation Planning Process for Air

The JFACC is responsible for planning joint air operations and uses the joint operation planning process for air (JOPPA) to develop a JAOP that guides employment of the air capabilities and forces made available to accomplish missions assigned by the JFC.

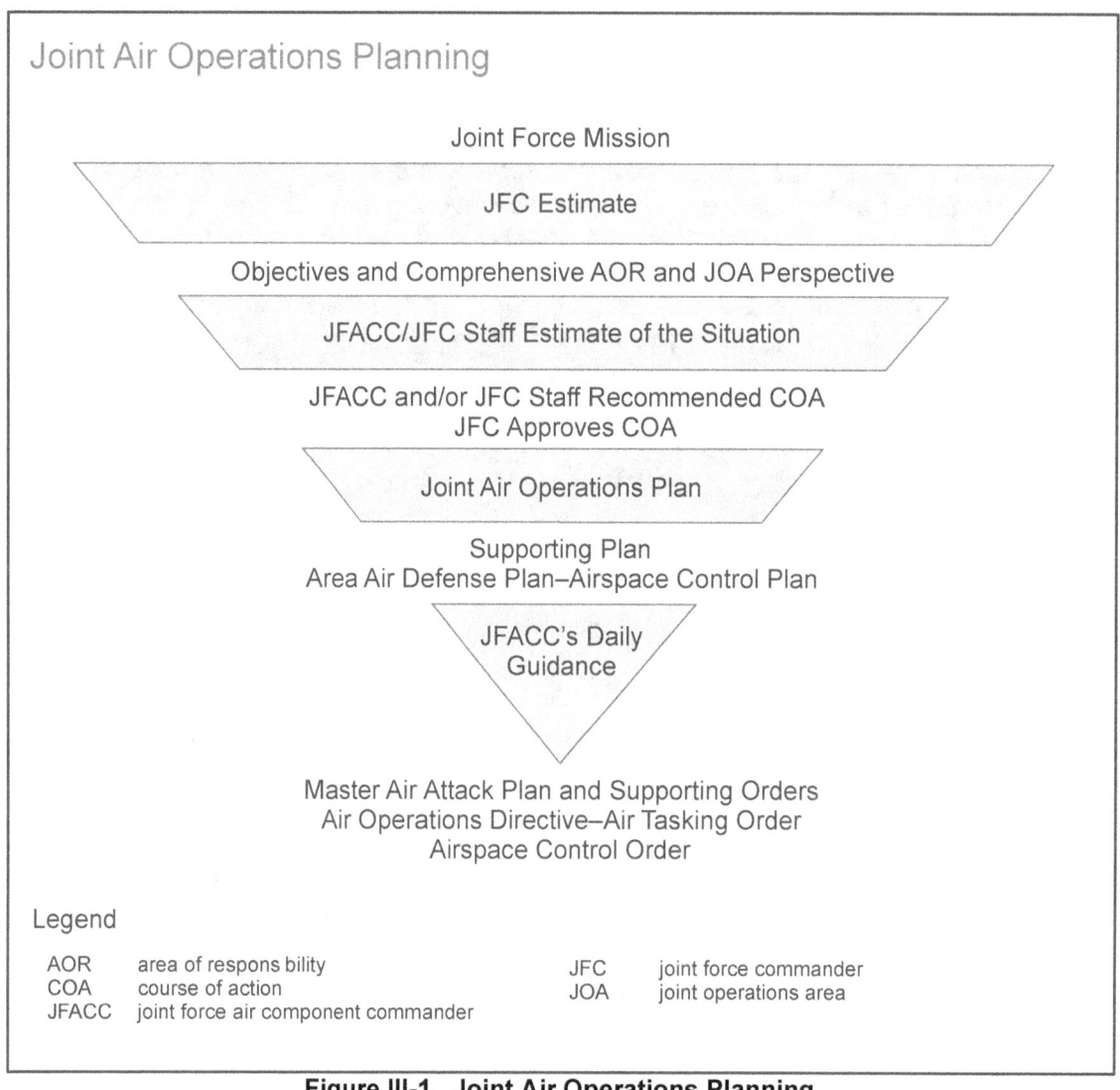

Figure III-1. Joint Air Operations Planning

a. **JFACC Planning Responsibilities.** The JFACC's role is to plan joint air operations. In doing so, the JFACC provides focus and guidance to the JAOC staff. The amount of direct involvement depends on the time available, preferences, and the experience and accessibility of the staff. The JFACC uses the entire staff during planning to explore the full range of adversary and friendly COAs and to analyze and compare friendly air capabilities with the adversary threat. **The JFACC must ensure that planning occurs in a collaborative manner with other components.** Joint air planners should meet on a regular basis with the JFC's planners and with planners from other joint force components to integrate operations across the joint force. Planning is a continuous process and only ends with mission accomplishment.

b. **The JAOP is the JFC's plan to integrate and coordinate joint air operations** and encompasses air capabilities and forces supported by, and in support of, other joint force components. The JFACC's planners must anticipate the need to make changes to plans (e.g., sequels or branches) in a dynamic and time-constrained environment. Planners should

---

Joint Air Estimate

Operational Description

- Purpose of the operation
- References
- Description of military operations

Narrative–Five Paragraphs

- Mission
- Situation and courses of action
- Analysis of opposing courses of action (adversary capabilities and intentions)
- Comparison of friendly courses of action
- Recommendation or decision

Remarks

- Remarks—Site plan identification number of the file where detailed requirements have been loaded into the Joint Operation Planning and Execution System

Figure III-2. Joint Air Estimate

include representatives from all components providing air capabilities or forces to enable their effective integration. Expertise requirements may include, but are not limited to, those listed in Figure III-3.

c. **JOPPA follows the joint operation planning process** found in JP 5-0, *Joint Operation Planning,* with specific details for joint air operations. JOPPA drives the production of the JAOP and supporting plans and orders. JOPPA may be utilized during deliberate planning, producing JAOPs that support OPLANs or concept plans. JOPPA may also be utilized as part of crisis action planning. It must always be tied closely to the overall joint planning being done by the JFC's staff and other Service or functional component staffs. While the steps are presented in sequential order, work on them can be concurrent or sequential. Nevertheless, the steps are integrated and the products of each step should be checked and verified for coherence and consistency. Figure III-4 illustrates the seven steps.

(1) **Step 1. Initiation**

(a) Planning is usually initiated by direction of a JFC, but the JFACC may initiate planning in anticipation of a planning requirement not directed by higher authority, but within the JFACC's authority. Joint air operations should be coordinated with all other relevant lines of operation (LOOs) and lines of effort (LOEs). Military air options are normally developed in combination with the other military and nonmilitary options so the JFC can appropriately respond to a given situation.

Example Subject Matter Expertise for Joint Air Planning

1. Logistics

2. Air mobility (airlift, air drop, and air refueling) planning

3. Targeting

4. Command and control

5. Intelligence, surveillance, and reconnaissance

6. Air and missile defense planning

7. Airspace control

8. Political-military affairs

9. Religious-cultural affairs

10. Information operations

11. Cyberspace operations

12. Space operations

13. Service and component liaisons

14. Weapon system capabilities

15. Mission planning/air tactics

16. Public affairs

17. Legal

18. Modeling and simulation

19. Electronic warfare, to include counter-improvised explosive device operations

20. Personnel recovery, to include combat search and rescue

21. Meteorological and oceanographic

22. Aeromedical evacuation/medical care

23. Administrative support

24. Munitions maintenance management

25. Counter chemical, biological, radiological, and nuclear planning

26. Force protection

Figure III-3. Example Subject Matter Expertise for Joint Air Planning

(b) The JFACC and staff perform an assessment of the initiating directive to determine how much time is available until mission execution, the current status of intelligence products and staff estimates, and other relevant factors that influence the planning situation. The JFC and JFACC typically provide initial guidance that may specify time constraints, outline initial coordination requirements, authorize movement of key capabilities within the commanders' authority, and direct other actions as necessary. The JFACC may produce an initial commander's intent during this step. Refer to Appendix A, "Sample Mission Statement and Commander's Intent," to see a sample JFACC mission statement and commander's intent.

Joint Operation Planning Process for Air

Step One: Initiation

The joint force air component commander (JFACC) and staff perform an assessment of the initiating directive to determine time available until mission execution, current status of intelligence products, and other factors relevant to the specific planning situation.

Step Two: Mission Analysis

Intelligence preparation of the battlespace (IPB) is initiated (if not already initiated). Adversary and friendly centers of gravity are analyzed. The joint force commander's mission and guidance are analyzed to produce the JFACC's mission and intent statements and planning guidance.

Step Three: Course of Action (COA) Development

IPB is refined to include adversary COAs. Multiple of COAs or one COA with significant branches and sequels are developed.

Step Four: COA Analysis and Wargaming

Friendly COAs are analyzed and wargamed against adversary COAs.

Step Five: COA Comparison

Wargaming results are used to compare COAs against predetermined criteria.

Step Six: COA Approval

Decision brief to the joint force commander (JFC) with COA recommendation. JFC selects COA.

Step Seven: Plan or Order Development

Selected COA is developed into a joint air operations plan and other orders, as appropriate

Figure III-4. Joint Operation Planning Process for Air

(2) **Step 2. Mission Analysis**

(a) Mission analysis is critical to ensure thorough understanding of the task and subsequent planning. It results in the JFACC's final mission statement that describes the joint air component's essential tasks. It should include the "who, what, when, where, and why" for the joint air operation, but seldom specifies "how." (See Figure III-5.) At the end of mission analysis, the JFACC should issue a commander's intent for the overall joint air operation, that is, the JFACC's contribution to the JFC's military end state. The JFACC's intent should express the end state to be produced by joint air operations and the purpose for producing them. It should also include the JFACC's assessment of where and how much risk is acceptable during the operation (see Figure III-6). Commanders intent is a concise expression of the purpose of the operation and the desired end state. While the commander's intent for the overall operation is needed at the end of mission analysis, the JAOP will eventually contain the commander's intent for each phase of the operation, and the AODs

Sample Joint Force Air Component Commander's
Mission Statement

When directed, the joint force air component commander (JFACC) will conduct joint air operations to deter aggression and protect deployment of the joint force.

Should deterrence fail, the JFACC, on order, will gain and maintain air superiority to enable joint operations within the operational area. Concurrently, the JFACC will support the joint force land component commander (JFLCC) in order to prevent enemy seizure of vital areas (to be specified).

On order, the JFACC, in conjunction with the JFLCC and joint force maritime component commander (JFMCC), will render enemy fielded military forces combat ineffective and prepare the operational environment for a counteroffensive. Concurrently, the JFACC will support the JFMCC in gaining and maintaining maritime superiority. The JFACC, on order, will support JFLCC and joint force special operations component commander ground offensive operations, degrade the ability of enemy national leadership to rule the country as directed, and destroy enemy weapons of mass destruction in order to restore territorial integrity, eliminate the enemy military threat to the region, support legitimate friendly government, and restore regional stability.

Figure III-5. Sample Joint Force Air Component Commander's Mission Statement

will contain the JFACC's intent for a specific ATO or period of time. Hence the commander's intent articulates a desired set of conditions for a given point in time and the purpose those conditions will support.

(b) Anticipation, prior preparation, and a trained staff are critical to timely mission analysis. Staff estimates generated during mission analysis are continually revisited and updated during the course of planning, execution, and assessment.

(c) Mission analysis includes developing a list of critical facts and assumptions. **Facts** are statements of known data concerning the situation. **Assumptions** are suppositions on the current situation or a presupposition on the future course of events, either or both assumed to be true in the absence of positive proof, necessary to enable the commander in the process of planning to complete an estimate of the situation and make a decision on the COA. Assumptions may also become commander's critical information requirements or drive the development of branch plans to mitigate the risks of a wrong assumption. Assumptions must be continually reviewed to ensure validity. Once an assumption is proven correct, it becomes a fact; or if proven incorrect, a new fact or

---

Sample Joint Force Air Component Commander's Intent Statement

- Purpose

  The purpose of this joint air operation will be initially to deter enemy aggression. Should deterrence fail, I will gain air superiority, render enemy fielded forces ineffective with joint airpower, degrade enemy leadership and offensive military capability as directed, and support joint group and special operations forces in order to restore territorial integrity and ensure the survival or restoration of legitimate government in a stable region.

- End State

  At the end state of this operation: Enemy military forces will be capable of limited defensive operations, will have ceased offensive action, and will have complied with war termination conditions. The succeeding state will retain no weapons of mass destruction capability; I will have passed air traffic control to local authorities, territorial integrity will be restored, and joint force air component commander operations will have transitioned to support of a legitimate and stable friendly government.

Figure III-6. Sample Joint Force Air Component Commander's Intent Statement

assumption is determined. They are necessary to enable a commander to complete an estimate of the situation, influence commander's critical information requirements, drive branch planning, and make decisions on COAs.

1. IPB should identify and analyze adversary and friendly centers of gravity (COGs) at the operational and tactical levels and contribute to the JIPOE. JIPOE is the analytical process used by joint intelligence organizations to produce intelligence assessments, estimates, and other intelligence products in support of the JFC's decision-making process. The process is used to analyze the physical domains; the information environment; political, military, economic, social, information, and infrastructure systems; and all other relevant aspects of the operational environment, and to determine an adversary's capabilities to operate within that environment. The IPB effort must be fully coordinated, synchronized, and integrated with the JIPOE effort of a joint intelligence center. A COG is a source of power that provides moral or physical strength, freedom of action, or will to act. In coordination with the JFC, the joint air component may focus on strategic and operational COGs as well as tactical-level details of adversary forces because air power can often directly or indirectly affect COGs through application of lethal and nonlethal force and through peaceful means.

See JP 2-01.3, Joint Intelligence Preparation of the Operational Environment, *for greater detail on JIPOE.*

2. The JFACC and staff prioritize the analyzed adversary and friendly critical vulnerabilities (CVs) associated with COGs based on their impact on achieving the objectives most effectively, in the shortest time possible, and at the lowest cost. The analyses of **adversary and friendly** CVs are incorporated into the various COAs considered during COA development.

(d) The JFACC, supported by the staff, determines the joint air objectives and the specified, implied, and essential tasks. The JFACC typically includes essential tasks in a mission statement. Essential tasks are specified or implied tasks that the JFACC must perform to accomplish the mission.

(e) The JFACC and staff examine readiness of all available air capabilities and forces to determine if there is enough capacity to perform all the specified and implied tasks. **The JFACC identifies additional resources needed for mission success to the JFC.** Factors to consider include available forces (including multinational contributions), command relationships (joint force, national, and multinational), force protection requirements, ROE, law of war, applicable treaties and agreements (including existing status of force agreements), base use (including land, sea, and air), overflight rights, logistic information (what is available in theater ports, bases, depots, war reserve material, host nation support), and what can be provided by other theaters and organizations.

(f) The **end state** is the set of required conditions that defines achievement of the commander's objectives and specific criteria for mission success. By articulating the joint air component's purpose, the JFACC provides an overarching vision of how the conditions at the end state support the joint operation and follow-on operations.

(3) **Step 3. COA Development**

(a) COA development is based on mission analysis and a creative determination of how the mission will be accomplished. The staff develops COAs. **A COA represents a potential plan the JFACC could implement to accomplish the assigned mission.** All COAs must meet the JFACC's intent and accomplish the mission.

(b) A COA consists of the following information: what type of military action will occur; why the action is required (purpose); who will take the action; when the action will begin and how long it will last (best estimate); where the action will occur; and how the action will occur (method of employment of forces). COAs may be broad or detailed depending on available planning time and JFACC's guidance. The staff should assess each COA to estimate its success against all possible adversary COAs. The staff converts the approved COA into a CONOPS. COA determination consists of four primary activities: COA development, analysis and wargaming, comparison, and approval. Air COAs will often require input from other component commanders to synchronize them with land and maritime operations.

(c) When time is limited, the JFACC should determine how many COAs the staff will develop and which adversary COAs to address. A complete COA should consider, at a minimum:

1. The JFACC's mission and intent (purpose and vision of military end state).

2. Desired end state.

3. Commander's critical information requirements.

4. C2 structure.

5. Essential tasks.

6. Available logistic support.

7. Available forces.

8. Available support from agencies and organizations.

9. Transition strategies between each phase.

10. Decision points.

(d) COAs should include the following specifics:

1. Operational and tactical objectives and effects and their related tactical tasks, in order of accomplishment.

2. Forces required and the force providers.

3. Force projection concept.

4. Employment concept.

5. Sustainment concept.

(e) The speed, range, persistence, and flexibility of air assets are their greatest advantages, and their employment location and purpose may change in minutes. Air strategists and planners deal with objective sequencing and prioritization, operational phasing, employment mechanisms, and weight of effort. In addition, COAs may vary by the phase in which an objective is achieved or the degree to which an objective is achieved in each phase.

(f) Air COAs may be presented in several ways. They may be presented as text and may discuss the priority and sequencing of objectives. Air COAs may also be depicted graphically—displaying weights of effort, phases, decision points, and risk. One helpful way to depict an air COA graphically is to depict it as one or more logical LOOs or LOEs, as described in JP 5-0, *Joint Operation Planning*. Any quantitative estimates and assessment criteria presented should clearly indicate common units of measurement in order to make valid comparisons between COAs. For example, a sortie is not a constant value for analysis—one F/A-18 sortie does not equate to one B-2 sortie. Air COAs should avoid numerical presentation. Ultimately, the JFACC will direct the appropriate style and content of the COA.

(g) The first step in COA development is to determine the measures that will accomplish the JFACC's mission and support achievement of the JFC's objectives. The framework of objectives, effects, and tasks provides a clear linkage of overall strategy to task. While the JFC normally provides operational objectives to the JFACC, they may also emerge through mission analysis or COA development, developed by the JFACC and the JAOC SD staff in consultation with the JFC. An objective should be clearly defined, decisive, and state an attainable goal. JFACC support to other components should also be expressed in terms of objectives. Resulting objectives can then be prioritized with other JFACC objectives in accordance with the JFC's CONOPS. **Supporting objectives should describe what aspect of the adversary's capability the JFC or other component wants to affect.** For example, the JFLCC's attack may require disrupting the enemy's operational reserve. Supporting JFACC objectives could be expressed as "render enemy's operational reserve unable to conduct counterattacks on JFLCC forces" or "destroy enemy's operational reserve's offensive capability." Clearly defined objectives prevent confusion over what the force is trying to accomplish and reduce the risk of mission failure.

(h) Commanders plan joint operations by developing objectives supported by measurable effects and assessment indicators. Analysis of effects (desired and undesired) and determination of measures of effectiveness (MOEs) during planning for joint air operations are usually conducted by the JAOC strategy plans and operational assessment teams, assisted by all other planning elements of the JAOC.

(i) To clarify, objectives *prescribe* friendly goals. Effects *describe* system behavior in the operational environment. Desired effects are the conditions related to achieving objectives. Tasks, in turn, *direct* friendly action. Objectives and effects are assessed through MOEs. Empirically verifiable MOEs may help ensure the JFACC knows when objectives have been achieved. Accomplishment of friendly tasks is assessed through measures of performance (MOPs). MOEs help answer questions like, "Are we doing the right things, or are alternative actions required?" MOEs also help focus component operational assessment efforts, inform processing, exploitation, and dissemination (PED) priorities, and identify ISR requirements. MOPs help answer questions like, "Are we doing things right: Were the tasks completed to standard?" Figure III-7 depicts the relationship of objectives, effects, and tasks and their associated assessment measures.

(j) Once strategists and planners define the joint air objectives and supporting effects and tasks, they further refine potential air COAs based on the objective priority, sequence, phasing, weight of effort, and matched resources. This is one method of differentiating COAs. Other methods include varying time available, anticipated adversary activities, friendly forces available, and higher-level guidance. For air planning, a single COA may be developed with several branches and sequels that react to possible adversary activities.

(k) **Planners should determine the validity of each air COA based on suitability, feasibility, acceptability, distinguishability, and completeness.**

(l) The relationship between resources and COA development is critical. **COA development must take into account the resource constraints of the joint force at large** (see Figure III-8). Competing requirements for limited airlift will often result in deployment orders less than ideal for all components but optimal for the joint force as a whole. The JFC must ensure the time-phased force and deployment data (TPFDD) reflects the priorities and

Linking Objectives, Effects, and Tasks Examples

Objective:	Gain and maintain air superiority over Sector X.
Effect 1:	Multinational air forces capable of conducting air operations over Sector X without prohibitive interference from Red counter-air forces.
MOE:	Proportion of multinational air missions ineffective due to prohibitive interference from Red counter-air forces.
Task:	Destroy all Red SAM radars covering Sector X.
MOP:	Proportion of known Red force SAM radars covering Sector X destroyed.
Task:	Degrade Red air C2 capacity by 90%.
MOP:	% of Red air C2 links severed.
Effect 2:	Coalition ground forces capable of conducting operations in Sector X without prohibitive interference from Red forces air or missile attack.
MOE:	% of coalition ground force phase objectives achieved without delay or losses from Red air or missile attack.
Task:	Destroy known fixed Red SRBM launch facilities within range of Sector X.
MOP:	Proportion of known Red SRBM launch facilities within range of Sector X destroyed.
Task:	Deny Red attack aircraft sortie generation.
MOP:	Proportion of Red attack airfields denied sortie generation capability.

Legend

C2	command and control	SAM	surface-to-air missile
MOE	measure of effectiveness	SRBM	short-range ballistic missile
MOP	measure of performance		

Figure III-7. Linking Objectives, Effects, and Tasks Examples

requirements of the joint force. Planners must ensure the COA developed adheres to deployment considerations across the force and does not assume away potential mobility and distribution system pitfalls.

(m) During air COA development, the **JFACC and staff help the commander identify risk areas that require attention.** These will vary based on the specific mission and situation and may be divided into two broad areas: combat support and operational considerations. Combat support includes TPFDD planning that will critically affect the joint force strategy and execution. Also considered with the TPFDD are basing, access, logistic support available, and force protection requirements (see Figure III-9). However, since TPFDD execution, basing, and logistic support are the responsibility of the JFC and Service components, the JFACC's planning effort needs to focus on the operational limitations imposed by them.

(n) Decisions related to operational assumptions may drive changes in how the JFACC operates. These changes range from JOPPA process changes to targeting and weaponeering methods. **One of the first considerations for the JFACC is air superiority.** The JFACC is responsible for considering the risk related to air defense planning when

```
Combat Support Considerations

  • Basing                              • Reachback

  • Force protection                    • Out of theater staging

  • Petroleum, oils, and lubricants     • Long-range assets
    availability
                                        • Sustainment (airlift and sealift)
  • Armaments/precision-guided
    munitions availability              • Communications systems

  • After-action report planning        • Aerial port and seaport of
                                          debarkation location
```

Figure III-8. Combat Support Considerations

designated as the AADC. The commander's operational assumptions will determine the resources committed, force posturing, and structure of the air and missile defense plan.

(o) The individual designated to be the JFACC may also be designated the SCA within a joint force to coordinate joint space operations and integrate space capabilities. This responsibility may entail the coordination and integration of the capabilities of other Services' and national agencies' space assets in order to maintain space superiority and exploit the space domain to create effects across the operational environment to achieve JFC objectives.   Space considerations should be fully integrated with operations in the operational environment, and should be fully incorporated into COA development.

(p) The JFC's assumptions will also affect the operational assumptions made by the joint force air strategists and planners. The joint force structure and campaign or OPLAN directly influence the JFACC's risk estimate and guidance.

```
Risk Management: Combat Support Factors

  • Time-phased force and        • Just-in-time logistic
    deployment data                considerations

  • Basing                       • Bandwidth

  • Regional access              • Host-nation support

  • Logistic support             • Communications networks

  • Airbase defense requirements • Force protection

  • Reachback operations
```

Figure III-9. Risk Management: Combat Support Factors

(q) Minimizing the risk of friendly fire and collateral damage are operational factors in risk management (see Figure III-10). **The commander must balance the potential for friendly fire and collateral damage with mission success.** When the risk becomes unacceptable, the commander should consider changes in operational employment.

(4) **Step 4. COA Analysis and Wargaming**

(a) **COA analysis involves wargaming each COA against the adversary's most likely and most dangerous COAs.** Wargaming is a recorded "what if" session of actions and reactions designed to visualize the flow of the conflict or operation and evaluate each friendly COA in the light of adversary adaptation. Wargaming is a valuable step in the planning process because it stimulates ideas and provides insights that might not otherwise be discovered. It also provides initial detailed planning while determining the strengths and weaknesses of each COA. This may alter or create a new COA based on unforeseen critical events, tasks, or problems identified. Wargaming is often a sequential process, but planning groups should adjust their wargame style based on JFACC guidance, time available, situation, and staff dynamics. Wargaming begins by assembling all the tools and information planners require and establishing the general rules to follow. Recording the activity is vital and directly contributes to identifying the advantages and disadvantages of a COA and providing sufficient detail for future JAOP development. Planners may use a synchronization matrix to detail the results of wargaming.

(b) Time permitting, the staff should:

<u>1.</u> Consider all facts and assumptions in each proposed COA and their possible effects on the action.

<u>2.</u> Consider active and passive measures to decrease the impact of adversary counteractions.

<u>3.</u> Consider conflict termination issues and the end state.

<u>4.</u> Think through one's own actions, adversary reactions, and friendly counteractions.

Risk Management: Operational Factors

- Joint force commander assumptions concerning the operation
- Friendly fire
- Collateral damage

- Force protection
- Information assurance
- Multinational considerations
- Command and control architecture

Figure III-10. Risk Management: Operational Factors

(c) COA analysis and wargaming conclude when planners have refined each plan in detail and identified the advantages and disadvantages of each air COA. Automation in the planning process and joint analysis centers may provide additional modeling support to wargaming, increasing the accuracy and speed of COA analysis.

(5) **Step 5. COA Comparison**

(a) Comparing air COAs against predetermined criteria provides an analytical method to identify the best employment options for air forces and capabilities. The same method used in JP 5-0, *Joint Operation Planning,* is used in air COA comparison.

(b) Another technique for air COA comparison involves developing an objective-risk timeline. LOOs and LOEs may help to elucidate the relationships between objectives, effects, time, and risk. In LOOs and LOEs, objectives, decisive points, or other significant events are plotted against a timeline that identifies when certain objectives or actions will occur. Risk for each air COA based on the LOO or LOE is identified. The resulting graphical representation may form the basis for the staff's recommendation and presentation to the JFACC.

(6) **Step 6. COA Approval.** The staff determines the best air COA to recommend to the commander. The staff presents their recommended air COA usually in the form of a briefing. This briefing includes a summary of the operational design and planning process that led to the recommended air COA. Ideally, the JFACC should be involved in the process, especially in the early operational design stages. Depending on the level of JFACC involvement and the degree of parallel planning the commander accomplishes, **air COA selection will vary from choosing among various alternatives to directly approving the staff-recommended air COA.** The air COA is identified, adjusted (if required), and selected by the JFACC for presentation to the JFC. Once the JFC approves an air COA, the JOPPA contributes directly to JAOP preparation.

(7) **Step 7. Plan or Order Development**

(a) For the joint air component, this step concentrates on the preparation of the JAOP. **The JAOP details how the joint air effort supports the JFC's overall operation or campaign plan.** JAOP development is a collaborative effort of the JFACC staff, the JFC staff, other joint force and Service component staffs, and outside agencies. Once the total force structure is determined, force availability, deployment, timing, basing availability, and sustainment requirements are matched with logistic and planning requirements. With this information, the JFACC's ability to accomplish the assigned mission is reevaluated and adjusted as necessary. The JAOP should accomplish the following:

1. **Integrate the efforts of joint air capabilities and forces and, where applicable and appropriate, space and cyberspace capabilities and/or support mechanisms/enablers.**

2. **Identify objectives, effects, and tasks.**

<u>3</u>. **Identify MOEs and indicators used to determine whether air operations are creating desired effects and achieving objectives.**

<u>4</u>. **Account for current and potential adversary COAs.**

<u>5</u>. **Integrate and synchronize the phasing of operations with the JFC's plan.**

<u>6</u>. **Indicate what capabilities and forces are required to achieve joint air objectives.** In addition to air capabilities and forces, planners should include land, maritime, space, cyberspace, and information-related capabilities required to meet joint air objectives.

<u>7</u>. **Develop specific procedures for allocating, tasking, exercising, and transitioning C2 of joint air capabilities and forces.**

(b) **In addition to building the plan for the employment of air forces,** the JAOP should also include considerations for phase transitions, decision points, conflict termination, redeployment (if applicable), and procedures to capture lessons learned. Incomplete planning for conflict termination and the end state can result in the waste of valuable resources, aggravate a tenuous peace, cause a return to hostilities, or lead to numerous other unintended consequences. The list of considerations for conflict termination is specific to each situation and is never formulated in a vacuum or without extensive consultations with national leadership. This part of the plan should also address the prospect of the "surge" of air forces to accomplish phases of the operation, based on projected operating tempo.

For information on the joint operation planning process, see JP 5-0, Joint Operation Planning.

4. Joint Targeting

a. **Targeting is the process of selecting and prioritizing targets and matching the appropriate response to them, considering operational requirements and capabilities.** Targeting is both a joint- and component-level function to create specific desired effects that achieve the JFC's objectives. Targeting selects targets that, when attacked, can create those effects, and selects and tasks the means to engage those targets. **Targeting is complicated by the requirement to deconflict** unnecessary duplication of target nominations **by different forces or different echelons within the same force and to integrate the attack of those targets with other components of the joint force.** An effective and efficient target development process coupled with the joint air tasking cycle is essential for the JFACC to plan and execute joint air operations. The joint targeting process should integrate the intelligence databases, analytical capabilities, and data collection efforts of national agencies, combatant commands, subordinate joint forces, and component commands.

b. The joint targeting cycle is an iterative process that is not time-constrained, and steps may occur concurrently, but it provides a helpful framework to describe the steps that must be satisfied to successfully conduct joint targeting. The deliberate and dynamic nature of the joint targeting process is adaptable through all phases of the air tasking cycle. As the situation changes and opportunities arise, steps of the joint targeting process can be accomplished quickly to create the commander's desired effects. **There are six phases to the joint targeting cycle: end state and commander's objectives, target development and prioritization, capabilities analysis, commander's decision and force assignment, mission planning and force execution, and assessment.**

For more detailed information on targeting and joint fires, see JP 3-60, Joint Targeting.

c. **Targeting mechanisms should exist at multiple levels.** The President, Secretary of Defense, or headquarters senior to JFCs may provide guidance, priorities, and targeting support. Joint force components identify requirements, nominate targets that are outside their operational area or exceed the capabilities of organic and supporting assets, and conduct execution planning. After the JFC makes final targeting decisions, components plan and execute assigned missions.

d. **Typically, the JFC organizes a joint targeting coordination board (JTCB).** The JTCB's focus is to develop broad targeting priorities and other guidance in accordance with the JFC's objectives as they relate operationally. The JFC normally appoints the deputy JFC or a component commander to chair the JTCB. If the JFC so designates, a JTCB may be an integrating center to accomplish broad targeting oversight functions or a JFC-level review mechanism to refine or approve the joint integrated prioritized target list (JIPTL). The JTCB needs to be a joint activity comprised of representatives from the staff, all components, and, as required, other agencies, multinational partners, and/or subordinate units.

e. **The JFC defines the role of the JTCB.** The JTCB provides a forum in which all components can articulate strategies and priorities for future operations to ensure they are integrated and synchronized. **The JTCB normally facilitates and coordinates joint force targeting activities with the components' schemes of maneuver to ensure that the JFC's priorities are met.** Targeting issues are generally resolved below the level of the JTCB, by direct coordination between elements of the joint force, but the JTCB and/or JFC may address specific targeting issues not previously resolved.

f. The JFC may also form a **joint fires element (JFE)** and/or a **joint targeting working group (JTWG), both of which aid coordination and integration of the joint targeting process.** The JFE is an optional staff element comprised of representatives from the JFC's J-3, the components, and other elements of the JFC staff. The JFE is an integrating staff element that synchronizes and coordinates fires planning and coordination on behalf of the JFC. The JTWG is an action-officer-level venue, typically chaired by the JFE chief, J-2 (chief of targets), or similar representative. The JTWG supports the JTCB by conducting initial collection, consolidation, and prioritization of targets and synchronization of target planning and coordination on behalf of the JFC.

See JP 3-60, Joint Targeting, for more information on the JTCB, JFE, and JTWG.

g. **The JFC will normally delegate the authority to conduct execution planning, coordination, and deconfliction associated with joint air targeting to the JFACC and**

will ensure that this process is a joint effort. The JFACC must possess a sufficient C2 infrastructure, adequate facilities, and ready availability of joint planning expertise. A targeting mechanism tasked with detailed planning, weaponeering, and execution is also required to facilitate the process.

h. The JFACC develops a JAOP that accomplishes the objectives directed by the JFC. **Integration, synchronization, deconfliction, allocation of air capabilities and forces, and matching appropriate weapons against target vulnerabilities are essential targeting functions for the JFACC.** National agencies, higher headquarters, JTFs, and task forces subordinate to the JFC, supporting unified commands, and functional/Service components may nominate targets to the JFC for processing and inclusion on the JIPTL through a target nomination list (TNL) (for additional details on TNL see JP 3-60, *Joint Targeting*). **Targets scheduled for attack by component air capabilities and forces should be included on an ATO for deconfliction and coordination.** All component commanders within the joint force should have a basic understanding of each component's mission and general scheme of maneuver. All components should provide the JFACC a description of their air plan to minimize the risk of friendly fire, assure deconfliction, avoid duplication of effort, and provide visibility to all friendly forces. This basic understanding allows for integration of targeting efforts between components and within the JFC staff and agencies.

5. **The Targeting Effects Team**

a. The JFACC may establish a targeting effects team (TET) as part of the JAOC. The TET's responsibilities are varied but key to the targeting process. The TET validates targets to be engaged by joint air forces per the JFC's targeting guidance, links targets to appropriate tactical tasks in the AOD, weaponeers targets to create desired effects, and verifies MOEs/MOPs. It also deconflicts and coordinates target nominations based on estimates of what targets can be attacked and provides other targeting support requiring component input at the JFACC level. If the JFC delegates joint targeting oversight authority to the JFACC, that commander should possess or have access to sufficient C2 infrastructure, adequate facilities, and joint planning expertise to effectively manage and lead the JFC's joint targeting operations. When the JFACC has JFC approval, the TET receives all target nominations (that cannot be addressed at lower echelon levels) and prioritizes them in accordance with the objectives and tactical tasks set forth in the AOD to form the draft JIPTL. Common organizational guidelines of the TET include the following:

(1) Chaired by the deputy JFACC or designated representative.

(2) Senior component liaison officers (LNOs) and key JFACC staff members comprise the TET.

(3) The JAOC CPD provides the staff support to the TET during the joint air tasking cycle.

b. **Draft JIPTL Construction.** The draft JIPTL is formed from a prioritized listing of targets based on JFC and component target priorities. To be a true integrated target list, the TET must present the JFACC with a draft JIPTL that includes targets and associated effects for engagement by both lethal and nonlethal means. In the case of a theater JFACC supporting multiple JFCs (e.g., two or more JTF commanders), the draft JIPTL should be constructed to meet the requirements of each supported JFC. Members consider the estimated available capabilities and their ability to engage the targets on the list. A draft JIPTL "cut line" is normally established. The draft JIPTL "cut line" should reflect which nominated targets will most likely be serviced (barring technical problems with aircraft, weather, retasking for higher priority targets, or other operational circumstances) with the projected apportionment of assets assigned or made available to the JFACC. Component LNOs and JAOC staff members should be ready to justify and/or prioritize target nominations among all the priorities of the joint operation. **The JFACC may also recommend to the JFC that additional assets from other components be used against targets on the draft JIPTL.** However, only the JFC can approve the use of other components' assets and forces. Close coordination must continue with the development of the JIPTL and with the development of the joint integrated prioritized collection list (JIPCL) to ensure effective and efficient use of assets that may be used to address targets on both the JIPTL and/or the JIPCL.

6. The Joint Air Tasking Cycle

a. The joint air tasking cycle provides for the effective and efficient employment of joint air capabilities and forces made available. This process provides an iterative, cyclic process for the planning, apportionment, allocation, coordination, and tasking of joint air missions and sorties within the guidance of the JFC. **The cycle accommodates changing tactical situations or JFC guidance as well as requests for support from other component commanders.** The joint air tasking cycle is an analytical, systematic cycle that **focuses joint air efforts on accomplishing operational requirements.** Much of the day-to-day tasking cycle is conducted through an interrelated series of information exchanges and active involvement in plan development, target development, air execution, and assessment (through designated component LNOs and/or messages), which provide a means of requesting and scheduling joint air missions. **A timely ATO is critical**—other joint force components conduct their planning and operations based on a prompt, executable ATO and are dependent on its information. Figure III-11 shows typical JFACC air tasking process responsibilities.

b. **The joint air tasking cycle begins with the JFC's objectives, incorporates guidance received during JFC and component coordination, and culminates with assessment of previous actions.** The ATO articulates the tasking for joint air operations for a specific execution timeframe, normally 24 hours. The joint air tasking cycle is synchronized with the JFC's battle rhythm. The JAOC normally establishes a 72- to 96-hour ATO planning cycle. The battle rhythm or daily operations cycle (schedule of events) articulates briefings, meetings, and report requirements. It provides suspense for targeting, AIRSUPREQs, friendly order of battle updates, etc., to produce the air battle plan (ABP) that includes the ATO message and other products. The battle rhythm is essential to ensure information is available when and where required to provide products necessary for the synchronization of joint air operations with the JFC's CONOPS and supporting other components' operations. Nonetheless, airpower must be responsive to a dynamic operational environment and the joint air tasking cycle must be flexible and capable of modification during ATO execution. The net result of the tasking process is a series of ATOs and related

Joint Force Air Component Commander
Air Tasking Process Responsibilities

- Plan, integrate, coordinate, allocate, task, and direct the joint air effort in accordance with the joint force commander's (JFC's) guidance and joint force objectives.

- Develop a joint air operations plan derived from the JFC's broader operation or campaign objective and guidance regarding the objectives, effects, tasks, and responsibilities of joint air capabilities and forces.

- After consulting with other component commanders, recommend apportionment of the joint air effort by priority that should be devoted to various air operations for a given period of time.

- Translate air apportionment into allocations and develop targeting guidance into the air operations directive and air tasking order.

- Direct and ensure deconfliction of joint air operations.

- Synchronize joint air operations with space and cyberspace operations.

- Coordinate with the appropriate components' agencies or liaison elements for integration and deconfliction with land and maritime operations.

- Coordinate with the appropriate components' agencies or liaison elements for tasking of the air forces and capabilities made available.

- Coordinate with the joint force special operations component commander's special operations liaison element for integration, synchronization, and deconfliction with special operations.

- Monitor execution and redirect joint air operations as required.

- Compile component target requirements and prioritize targets based on JFC guidance, if delegated the responsibility.

- Accomplish tactical and operational assessment.

**Figure III-11. Joint Force Air Component Commander Air Tasking
Process Responsibilities**

products in various stages of progress at any time (see Figure III-12). The primary factor that drives the daily schedule for the development of the ATO is the battle rhythm. The battle rhythm is a very detailed timeline that lists series of briefings, meetings, etc., to produce specific products by a specified time.

c. The full joint air tasking cycle, from JFC guidance to the start of ATO execution, is dependent on the JFC's and JFACC's procedures. A 72-hour cycle, starting with objectives, effects, and guidance is fairly standard. The precise timeframes should be specified in the JFC's OPLAN or the JFACC's JAOP. Long-range combat air assets positioned outside the theater but operating in the JOA may be airborne before ATO publication or execution. These assets require the most current ATO information and updates. The JAOC, however, possesses the capability to retask such missions even during execution. Intertheater air mobility missions may not necessarily operate within the established tasking cycle. The AMD is an AOC division that assists the CPD with intertheater and intratheater air mobility missions that should be integrated into the ATO.

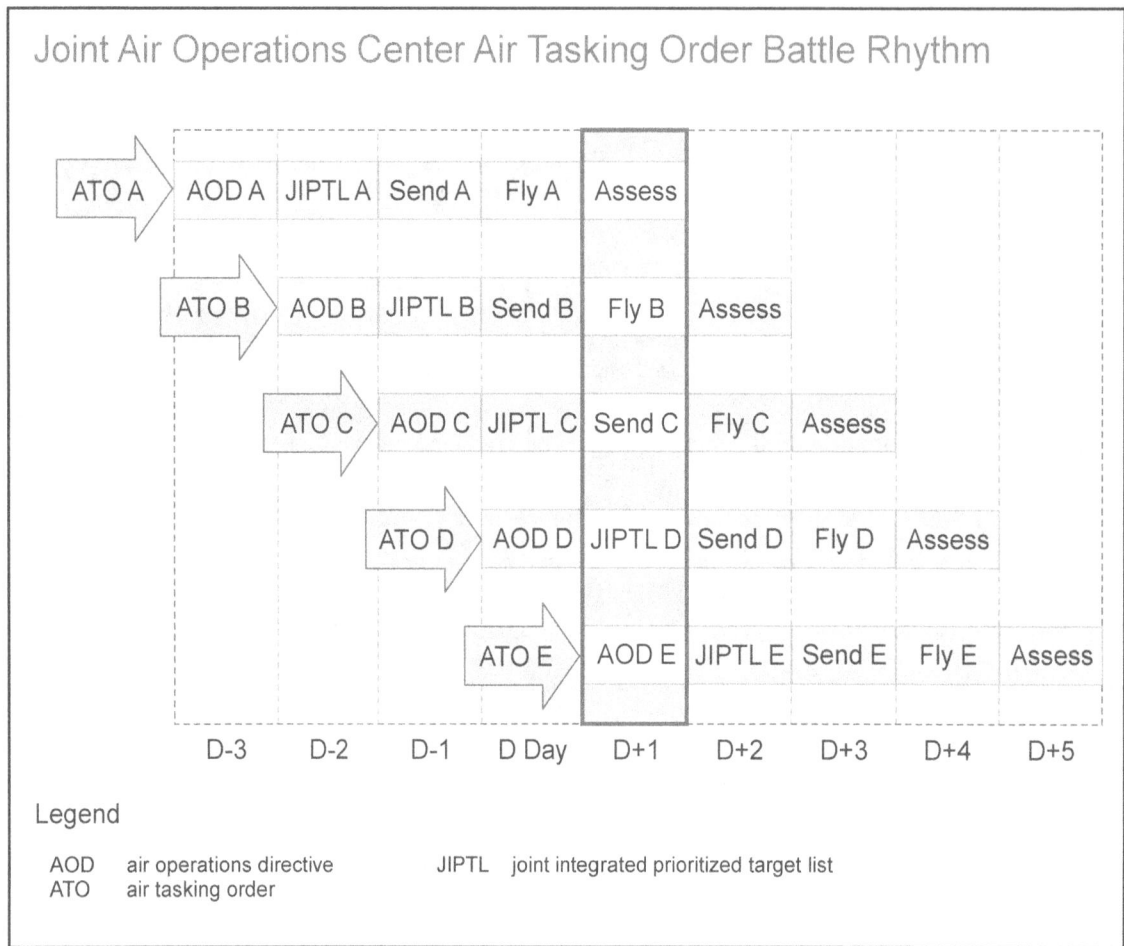

Figure III-12. Joint Air Operations Center Air Tasking Order Battle Rhythm

d. The ATO matches and tasks air forces and capabilities made available to the JFACC for tasking to prosecute targets and resource AIRSUPREQs and other requirements. Other component air missions should be on the ATO to improve joint force visibility and to assist with overall coordination and deconfliction. The other component air missions that appear on the ATO may not be under the control of the JFACC, and the JFACC will coordinate changes with all affected components.

e. **Joint Air Tasking Cycle Stages.** The joint air tasking cycle consists of six stages (Figure III-13). The joint air tasking cycle receives products from information developed during the joint targeting cycle and other joint force processes. Both the joint targeting cycle and joint air tasking cycle are systematic processes to match available capabilities and forces with specific targets to achieve the JFC's objectives. Unlike the joint targeting cycle, the joint air tasking cycle is time-dependent, built around finite time periods to plan, prepare for, and conduct joint air operations. There is a set suspense for product inputs and outputs for each stage of the joint air tasking cycle. **Prior to the JFC and component commanders' meeting, the JFACC should meet with senior component liaisons and the JFC's staff to develop recommendations on joint air planning and apportionment for future operations.** (The use of the term "meeting" is notional; other methods of information exchange can also be used.) This meeting may review JFC objectives and guidance, assess

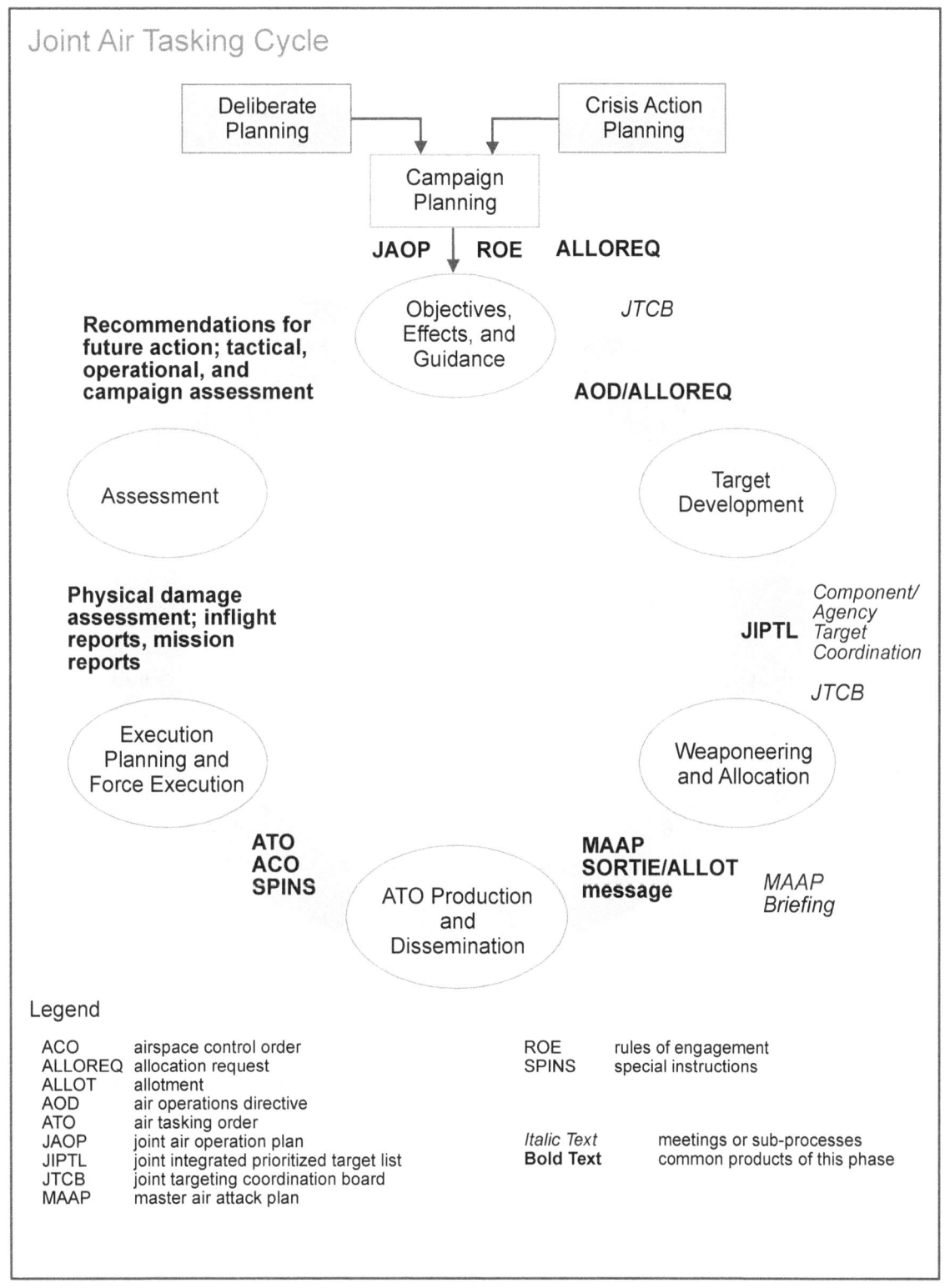

Figure III-13. Joint Air Tasking Cycle

and analyze results of joint force operations and consider changes to ongoing joint air operations; review adversary capabilities and COAs, COGs, decisive points, CVs, and key targets, and discuss updates to the JIPTL, based on JFC guidance. The JFACC should provide objectives and guidance to the staff for joint air operations to achieve the JFC's intent, recommend an air scheme of maneuver, review joint force capabilities and forces available to achieve assigned tasks, refine requirements for capabilities and forces from other components, and, in consultation with other component commanders, formulate an air apportionment recommendation for presentation to the JFC.

(1) **Stage 1: Objectives, Effects, and Guidance**

(a) The JFC consults often with component commanders to assess the results of the joint force's efforts and to discuss the strategic direction and future plans. This provides component commanders an opportunity to make recommendations, make support requirements known, and state their ability to support other components. The JFC provides updates to the guidance, priorities, and objectives based on enemy operations and the current/expected friendly order of battle. The JFC also refines the intended CONOPS. **The JFC's guidance on objectives and effects will identify targeting priorities and will include the JFC's air apportionment decision.**

(b) **Air Apportionment. Air apportionment allows the JFC to ensure the priority of the joint air effort is consistent with campaign or operation phases and objectives.** Given the many functions that joint air forces can perform, its operational area-wide application, and its ability to rapidly shift from one function to another, JFCs pay particular attention to air apportionment. **After consulting with other component commanders, the JFACC makes the air apportionment recommendation to the JFC.** The methodology the JFACC uses to make the recommendation may include priority or percentage of effort devoted to assigned mission-type orders, JFC objectives, or other categories significant to the campaign or operation. The air apportionment recommendation is a vital part of the joint air planning and tasking process. The JAOC SD formulates the air apportionment recommendation that the JFACC submits to the JFC for upcoming iterations of the joint tasking cycle. With air capabilities made available to the JFACC, the strategy plans team can recommend the relative level of effort and priority that may be applied to various JFC and/or JFACC objectives. The end result is an air apportionment recommendation. This product is normally forwarded to the JTCB for coordination and approval by the JFC. In the case of a theater JFACC supporting multiple JFCs (e.g., two or more JTF commanders), the air apportionment recommendation (e.g., CAS, interdiction) referenced here is made to each supported JFC. The JFC is the final approval authority for the air apportionment decision.

(2) **Stage 2: Target Development.** This is the point in the joint targeting cycle and intelligence process, after analysts from other organizations have incorporated all-source intelligence reports into a targeting database, where efforts of the joint air targeting cycle relate target development to air tasking and target aimpoints are selected, and these and other data are submitted to the TET. The TET correlates target nominations to the tactical tasks in the AOD for that ABP period. It screens nominated targets, ensuring that once attacked they create the desired effects that meet JFC guidance as delineated in the AOD, and verifies that

chosen MOEs will accurately evaluate progress and can be collected against. It prioritizes nominated targets based on the best potential for creation of the JFC's desired effects and components' priorities and timing requirements. The product of this effort, when approved by the JFC or the JFC's designated representative (e.g., JTCB), is the JIPTL.

(3) **Stage 3: Weaponeering and Allocation**

(a) During this stage, **JAOC personnel quantify the expected results of the employment of lethal and nonlethal means against prioritized targets to create desired effects.** The JIPTL provides the basis for weaponeering assessment activities. All approved targets are weaponeered, to include recommended aimpoints, weapon systems and munitions, fusing, target identification and description, desired direct effects of target attack, probability of creating the desired effect, and collateral damage concerns. **The final prioritized targets are developed and are then provided to the master air attack plan (MAAP) team.** The TET may provide the MAAP team a draft JIPTL to begin initial planning. Once the JIPTL is approved by the JFC, the MAAP team can finalize force allocation (sortie flow plan). The force application cell can complete coordination with the supporting force enhancement cell to satisfy mission requirements to ensure the prioritized targets are planned to generate effects to achieve objectives while maximizing the combat effectiveness of joint air assets. **The resulting MAAP is the plan for employment that forms the foundation of the ATO.** The MAAP is normally a graphic depiction of capabilities required for a given period. The development of the MAAP includes review of JFC and JFACC guidance, component plans and their AIRSUPREQs, updates to targets, availability of capabilities and forces, target selection from the JIPTL, and weapon system allocation. Components may submit critical changes to targets, AIRSUPREQs and asset availability during the final stages of ATO development. The completed MAAP matches available resources to the prioritized target list. It accounts for air refueling requirements, suppression of enemy air defenses requirements, air defense, ISR, and other factors affecting the plan.

(b) **Air Allocation.** Following the JFC's air apportionment decision, **the JFACC translates that decision into total number of sorties by weapon system type available for each objective and task.** Based on the apportionment decision, internal requirements, and AIRSUPREQ messages, each air-capable component prepares an allocation request (ALLOREQ) message for transmission to the JFACC (normally not less than 36 hours prior to the start of the ATO execution period, thus coinciding with the beginning of the MAAP process). ALLOREQ messages report (from other components to the JFACC):

1. Number and type of air assets made available for tasking as directed by the JFC air apportionment decision. These may be excess sorties not required by the air-capable components and made available for tasking by the JFACC. The air capable component commander will normally direct what missions those assets are capable of conducting.

2. Includes requests for air support from components to the JFACC that exceed the unit's capabilities.

(c) **Allotment.** The sortie allotment (SORTIEALOT) message confirms (and where necessary modifies) the ALLOREQ and provides general guidance to plan joint air operations. The JAOC reviews each component's allocation decision/ALLOREQ message and may prepare a SORTIEALOT message back to the components as required, in accordance with established operations plans guideline. The SORTIEALOT addresses three basic requirements:

1. Revisions, if any, to the component's planned allocation of joint air sorties necessitated by unforeseen joint force requirements and within the JFC's air apportionment guidance.

2. Approval/disapproval of component requests and allotment of other component's excess sorties.

3. Revisions to mission data for component AIRSUPREQs.

(4) **Stage 4: ATO Production and Dissemination.** ATO production team constructs, publishes, and disseminates the daily ATO and applicable SPINS to appropriate forces. ATO production team is responsible for the dissemination of the ATO. They develop and maintain a comprehensive address list of approved ATO recipients and coordinate redundant procedures for timely ATO dissemination and receipt. The air operations database (AODB) manager is an experienced ATO production technician who oversees the AODB update and change process. The AODB consists of the friendly order of battle that includes bases, units, aircraft, mission types, call signs, etc., and incorporates the identification friend or foe/selective identification feature plan. JFC and JFACC guidance, including the AOD; target worksheets; the MAAP; and component requirements are used to finalize the ATO, SPINS, and ACO. **Planners must develop airspace control and air defense instructions in sufficient detail to allow components to plan and execute all air missions listed in the ATO.** These directions must enable combat operations without undue restrictions, balancing combat effectiveness with the safe, orderly, and expeditious use of airspace. Instructions must provide for quick coordination of task assignment and reassignment (redirection, retargeting, or change of type of mission) and must direct aircraft identification and engagement procedures and ROE appropriate to the nature of the threat. These instructions should also consider the volume of friendly and possibly neutral air traffic, friendly air defense requirements, identification-friend-or-foe technology, weather, and adversary capabilities. Instructions are contained in SPINS and in the ACO, and are updated as frequently as required. The AOD, ATO, ACO, and SPINS provide operational and tactical direction at appropriate levels of detail. The level of detail should be very explicit when forces operate from different bases and multi-component or composite missions are tasked. In contrast, less detail is required when missions are tasked to a single component or base.

(5) **Stage 5: Execution Planning and Force Execution. The JFACC directs the execution of air capabilities and forces made available for joint air operations.** Inherent in this is the authority to redirect joint air assets. The JFACC will coordinate with affected component commanders upon redirection of joint sorties previously allocated for support of component operations. **Aircraft or other capabilities and forces not apportioned for**

joint air operations, but included in the ATO for coordination purposes, may be redirected only with the approval of the respective component commander or JFC. Aircraft or other capabilities and forces made available for joint air operations may be redirected with the approval of the JFACC.

(a) **The JAOC must be responsive to required changes during the execution of the ATO.** In-flight reports, discovery of time-sensitive targets (TSTs), and initial assessment (such as battle damage assessment [BDA]) may cause a redirecting of joint air capabilities and forces before launch or a redirection once airborne.

(b) During execution, **the JAOC is the focal point for changes to the ATO and is the centralized control node for tasking of joint air capabilities and forces.** It is also charged with coordinating and deconflicting those changes with the appropriate control agencies and components.

NOTE: Care must be taken when redirecting sorties from one target to another to ensure the proper weapons and fuses are available for the new target.

(c) Due to operational environment dynamics, **the JFACC may be required to make changes to planned joint air operations during execution.** Employment of joint air assets against emerging targets requires efficient, timely information sharing and decision making among components. It is critical that procedures be established, coordinated, and promulgated by the JFC before operations begin. **The dynamic targeting portion of the joint targeting cycle is established to facilitate this process.** The JFACC will coordinate with affected component commanders to ensure deconfliction of targets and to ensure those forces are out of danger relative to the new target area(s).

(d) **During execution, the JFACC is responsible for redirecting joint air assets to respond to moving targets or changing priorities.** Ground or airborne C2 platform mission commanders may be delegated authority from the JFACC to redirect sorties or missions made available to higher priority targets. It is essential, however, that the JAOC be notified of all redirected missions.

(6) **Stage 6: Assessment. Assessment is performed by all levels of the joint force.**

(a) The JFC should establish a dynamic system to conduct assessment throughout the joint force and to ensure that all components are contributing to the overall joint assessment effort. Normally, the joint force J-3 is responsible for coordinating assessment, assisted by the J-2. Assessment is a continuous process that measures the overall effectiveness of employing joint force capabilities during military operations. It determines progress toward accomplishment of tasks, creation of effects, and achievement of objectives. **The JFACC should continuously plan and evaluate the results of joint air operations and provide assessments to the JFC for consolidation into the overall assessment of the current operation.**

(b) Within the joint force, assessment is conducted at both the tactical and operational levels. At the tactical level, assessment is essential to decision making during

ATO execution. However, the tactical assessment process continues over days or weeks to evaluate the effectiveness of weapons and tactical engagements as additional information and analysis become available from sources within and outside the operational area. This should also include a determination of actual collateral damage. Air planners should determine MOPs to evaluate task accomplishment and MOEs to assess changes in system behavior, capability, or the operational environment. Planners should ensure that they establish logical links between air objectives and tasks and the measures used to evaluate them early in the planning sequence. They should also ensure that they identify intelligence collection management and other intelligence collection requirements as part of the planning process. **At the operational level, assessment is concerned with gathering information on the broader results achieved by air operations and planning for future operations.**

(c) In general, the assessment process at the tactical level provides one of the major sources of information for performing assessment at the operational level. Tactical inputs, along with a wide assortment of other information, aid in the development of the air component's operational-level assessment.

(d) The JFACC's operational-level assessment should be forwarded to the joint force J-3 as one component's input to the JFC's overall determination of the operation's success. Operational-level assessment can also serve as the basis for important recommendations that can affect the JFC's apportionment decision and the JFACC's allocation of air resources.

(e) Although assessment appears to mark the end of the air tasking cycle, it is an ongoing activity that provides important inputs to decision making and aiding processes throughout that cycle.

SECTION B. OTHER CONSIDERATIONS

7. Intelligence, Surveillance, and Reconnaissance Considerations

a. The GCC (theater J-2) may retain collection management authority (CMA) to establish, prioritize, and validate theater collection requirements, establish sensor tasking guidance, and develop theater-wide collection policies. CMA may reside at the JTF level or may be delegated to components. The theater J-2 retains full management authority (i.e., to validate, to modify, or to nonconcur) over all intelligence collection requirements within the AOR. The JFC's J-2 and J-3 jointly develop an overall collection strategy and posture for the execution of the ISR mission. The joint force J-2 reviews, validates, and prioritizes all intelligence requirements for the JFC. Users requesting airborne ISR support should make a concerted effort to request a clear identification of their required information or ISR product and not a specific ISR platform to perform a mission. For example, many different aircraft can provide imagery and data. Depending on the request, there might be more than one type of asset available to support a mission. Airborne ISR aircraft are typically high demand assets due to mission duration, and the ability to quickly respond to TST requests, and their ability to support multiple users. Retasking an airborne ISR asset during mission execution must be carefully considered. Dynamic retasking of ISR assets should be done by the appropriate commander after evaluating the full impacts of diverting the capability from the current mission and the impact to operational success or consequences without the asset. Dynamic ISR retasking priorities and procedures must be clearly specified in the ROE and SPINS.

b. **The JFACC will normally be the supported commander for the airborne ISR effort.** The JFC will normally delegate collection operations management for joint airborne ISR to the JFACC to authoritatively direct, schedule, and control collection operations for use by the J-2 in associated processing, exploitation, and reporting. The JAOC should request ISR support from the JFC or another component if available assets cannot fulfill specific airborne ISR requirements. It is imperative the JFACC remains aware of all surveillance and reconnaissance capabilities that can be integrated into joint air operations. ISRD collection managers build a daily collection plan, the reconnaissance, surveillance, and target acquisition annex, as a commonly understood plan which tasks airborne ISR platforms sensors and PED nodes. This product is an annex to the ATO and is available to the entire joint force. It is completed by ISR personnel in the MAAP.

c. National and non-DOD ISR resources are not normally placed under the JFC's OPCON. These resources may provide direct support to the JFC or one of the components, either full-time or on-call, but are normally shared with other commands or components. The supported commander will be provided with liaison teams upon request. These teams will normally be the points of contact for coordinating their specific ISR resources and associated capabilities with the supported commander's ISR operators. ISR operators forward the requirements to the appropriate command authority for approval.

d. ISR personnel are integrated into the JAOC. The complexity of integrating airborne ISR will normally determine whether the function is handled by a specialty team, cell, or division within the JAOC. The JFACC's ISR collection managers and operations planners will work with the joint force staff and other components to effectively coordinate national and theater ISR objectives. The ISR collection elements will manage and satisfy the JFACC's information requirements.

e. The JFACC provides integrated airborne ISR for the JFC. The JAOC provides the force integrated information from the JFACC's available airborne ISR support.

See JP 2-01, Joint and National Intelligence Support to Military Operations, *for further information.*

f. ISR systems undergoing the acquisition and research and development process, particularly the advanced concept technology demonstration phase, are normally requested through military development organizations and involve the applicable contractor. In such cases, the contractor is often requested to provide technical representatives in the JAOC and/or at the national or theater intelligence agency.

8. Air Mobility Considerations

a. Air mobility missions are integral to the success of joint operations. **Airlift is critical for deployment, redeployment, airdrop, AE, and sustainment, while aerial refueling is critical to deployment, redeployment, sustainment, and employment of air operations.**

AE is the most expeditious method of patient movement. The Commander, USTRANSCOM, normally retains OPCON of intertheater air mobility assets due to their global mission and nature. A support relationship is established between CCDRs. Intratheater airlift and theater refueling assets may be attached to a JTF, with OPCON normally delegated down to the appropriate Service component commander (usually the COMAFFOR). Integrating air mobility planning into the JAOP and monitoring mission execution is normally the responsibility of the AMD chief supported by a team of mobility specialists in the JAOC.

b. The DIRMOBFOR is normally a senior officer who is familiar with the AOR and possesses an extensive background in air mobility operations. The DIRMOBFOR may be sourced from the theater's organizations or from USTRANSCOM. Operationally, the DIRMOBFOR exercises coordinating authority for air mobility with commands and agencies within and external to the joint force. Specifically, the DIRMOBFOR coordinates with the JFACC's JAOC, Air Mobility Command's 618 Operations Center Tanker Airlift Control Center, and joint movement center (JMC)/joint deployment and distribution operations center (JDDOC) to expedite the resolution of air mobility issues. Additionally, the DIRMOBFOR, when designated, advises the JFACC and JAOC director, and assists the AMD chief, to ensure the effective integration of intertheater and intratheater air mobility operations, and facilitates intratheater air mobility operations. While the DIRMOBFOR should be collocated with the AMD to maximize effectiveness, the JAOC AMD remains under control of the JAOC director who manages execution of air mobility operations for the JFACC through the AMD chief.

c. **DIRMOBFOR also has distinct responsibilities in relation to JFC staffs.** Air mobility requirements do not originate in the JAOC. They originate at the component level and are validated by either the JDDOC, the theater JMC (when established), or by the GCC's J-3 in coordination with the logistics directorate of a joint staff (J-4). This may vary slightly in different theaters. Consequently, **an essential role for the DIRMOBFOR is to serve as the principal interface between the JAOC, the theater's J-4, and the JMC/JDDOC** to ensure appropriate prioritization of air mobility tasks while balancing requirements and air mobility capability.

d. When a JTF is formed, command relationships for air mobility forces will be established in accordance with the Unified Command Plan and the Global Force Management process. Command of these forces will be as established by the JFC and normally exercised through the COMAFFOR and/or JFACC with the advice and assistance of the DIRMOBFOR. The JAOC director is charged with the effectiveness of joint air operations and focuses on planning, coordinating, allocating, tasking, executing, and assessing air operations in the operational area based on JFACC guidance and DIRMOBFOR coordination. While the JAOC director provides direction principally to the JAOC's strategy, combat plans, and CODs, the DIRMOBFOR's focus is on the AMD and its primary components. Figure III-14 illustrates the arrangement of the JAOC and associated command relationships with respect to air mobility operations.

For more detailed information, see JP 3-17, Air Mobility Operations.

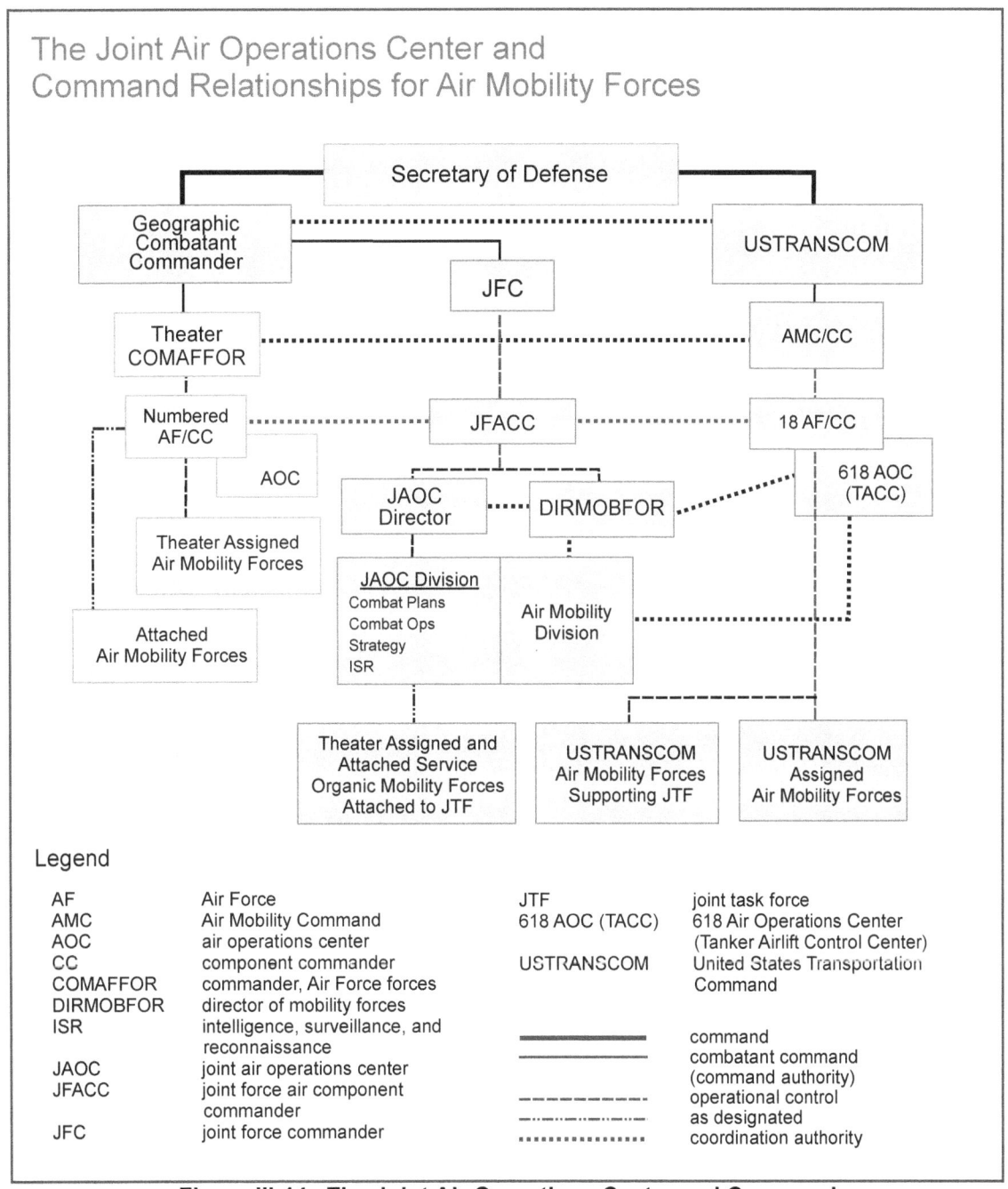

Figure III-14. The Joint Air Operations Center and Command Relationships for Air Mobility Forces

9. Unmanned Aircraft Systems Considerations

a. **General Considerations. UASs should be treated similarly to manned systems with regard to the established doctrinal warfighting principles.** Like manned aircraft, the operation of a UAS should adhere to the guidance contained in this publication. While the JFC retains the authority to determine the use and control of UAS forces, there are some unique issues for planners and commanders to consider when employing these systems. UAS technology can provide commanders with critical capabilities (CCs) to enhance their situational awareness to make informed decisions, protect forces, reduce collateral damage, and achieve objectives (see Figure III-15).

Note: The USAF refers to some of its larger UAS as remotely piloted aircraft to differentiate its operators who have been trained to similar standards as manned aircraft pilots.

b. **Unique Characteristics Associated with C2 of UASs**

(1) While the C2 processes for UASs are similar to those for manned assets, **several characteristics of UASs can make C2 particularly challenging:**

(a) UAS communication links are generally more critical than those required for manned systems. In the event of lost communications, a manned aircraft will typically

Unmanned Aircraft Systems Categorization Chart

UA Category	Maximum Gross Takeoff Weight (lbs)	Normal Operating Altitude (ft)	Speed (KIAS)	Representative UAS
Group 1	0-20	< 1200 AGL	100 kts	WASP III, TACMAV RQ-14A/B, Buster, Nighthawk, RQ-11B, FPASS, RQ16A, Pointer, Aqua/Terra Puma
Group 2	21-55	< 3500 AGL	< 250	ScanEagle, Silver Fox, Aerosonde
Group 3	< 1320	< 18,000 MSL	< 250	RQ-7B Shadow, RQ-15 Neptune, XPV-1 Tern, XPV-2 Mako
Group 4	> 1320	< 18,000 MSL	Any Airspeed	MQ-5B Hunter, MQ-8B Fire Scout, MQ-1C Gray Eagle, MQ-1A/B/C Predator
Group 5	> 1320	> 18,000 MSL	Any Airspeed	MQ-9 Reaper, RQ-4 Global Hawk, RQ-4N Triton

Legend

AGL	above ground level	lbs	pounds
FPASS	force protection aerial surveillance system	MSL	mean sea level
ft	feet	TACMAV	tactical micro air vehicle
KIAS	knots indicated airspeed	UA	unmanned aircraft
kts	knots	UAS	unmanned aircraft system

Figure III-15. Unmanned Aircraft Systems Categorization Chart

continue the mission and/or return safely to a home base or alternate field. Although UASs can be programmed to return to base upon loss of communication, they rely on a nearly continuous stream of communications (for both flight control and payload) to successfully complete a mission. Therefore, **communications security, specifically bandwidth protection (from both friendly interference and adversary action), is imperative.**

(b) UASs may be capable of transferring control of the aircraft and/or payloads to multiple operators while airborne. Clear transfer of authority and close coordination amongst all potential operators is required.

(c) Most larger UASs have **considerably longer endurance times** than comparable manned systems. Planners must exploit this capability when tasking UAS assets.

(d) Compliance with the ACO is critical. Unlike manned aircraft, UASs cannot typically "see and avoid" other aircraft. Additionally, UASs generally have small radar and visual signatures, and may not have identification, friend, or foe capability.

(e) A supporting UAS LNO/subject matter expert can facilitate the flow of information between UAS operators and the supported unit to ensure the supported unit understands UAS capabilities and limitations.

(f) Depending on the type of UAS and mission being conducted, planners and operators may have to consider the weather in four separate and widely dispersed locations (satellite relay, launch and recovery base, transit route(s), and anticipated target location). Weather considerations should also include solar activity, which may adversely impact high frequency and ultrahigh frequency and satellite communications.

(g) Some larger UASs may be employed using remote split operations (RSO). RSO refers to the geographical separation of the launch and recovery crew from the mission crew who employ the aircraft at a location other than where the aircraft is based. Key considerations for RSO include:

1. The forward logistics footprint may be reduced and expose fewer personnel to enemy actions by keeping associated support equipment and personnel external to the operational area. This may also require fewer forward base facilities.

2. Faster deployment/redeployment may be possible since only the launch and recovery crews, maintenance support, and equipment need to be moved forward (assuming communication infrastructure is available).

3. The network architecture may be more easily leveraged to support dissemination. Adding additional aircraft may require only minor routing configuration changes.

c. **Mission Planning Considerations.** Current doctrinal planning considerations for manned aircraft are generally applicable to UASs.

(1) **Allocation and tasking of UASs in Joint Operations.** The JFC process for determining what UASs to allocate to the JFACC will be no different than for the manned aircraft allocation decision process. Transferring C2 of UASs within a Service or functional component can be accomplished through Service or functional command structures.

(2) **C2 of theater-capable UASs.** Theater-capable UASs are able to range the theater of operations and/or support multiple users. They can be used to support the JFC (UASs made available by component commanders), a component commander's operations (organic UASs), or in support of other component commanders. As these low density assets can be in high demand, careful consideration must be made by the JFC and JFACC when making apportionment and allocation decisions. The JFC should attempt to meet the organic needs of the component commanders, while ensuring the JFACC has the assets available to execute JFC assigned JOA-wide operations. These decisions will typically change as the phase of an operation changes. As with any joint capable asset, the JFC retains the authority to use any UAS asset to meet the needs of the JFC mission. How theater-capable UAS operations are managed and planned will vary based on the type and phase of an operation.

(3) **Flight Planning.** All UA flights, regardless of the size of the UA, the mission profile, or the flight location, must follow approved planning, guidance, and procedures as prescribed in the AOD, ACO, ATO, and SPINS. Typically, it is not necessary to include Group 1 UAS on the ATO **unless their planned operating altitude is such that it could cause a conflict with other airborne operations.** All other UAS (Groups 2-5) shall be included in the ACO, ATO, and SPINS.

(4) **UAS Emergency Planning.** The unique requirements of UAS data links require detailed planning for lost link and emergency recoveries. UAS emergency procedures may be more complicated than those of manned platforms. Detailed planning for lost link; lost positioning, navigation, and timing (PNT) self-awareness (typically due to Global Positioning System [GPS] signal interference); and other emergency procedures and recoveries are required due to the dependence on PNT information and the control data link. Planned lost link and emergency profiles must be safe and consistent with all airspace requirements, follow ACO guidance, and deconflict with other airspace users. Emergency planning must also consider the potential for recovery of armed UA into an emergency divert base. The divert base must incorporate a compatible launch and recovery element to ensure safe UA recovery.

d. **Employment Considerations.** Effective UAS employment requires an in-depth knowledge of theater SPINS, ROE, ACP, ACO, and ATO, as well as UAS capabilities and limitations.

(1) **Factors to Consider When Tasking UASs.**

(a) Users requesting support should differentiate their request as either ISR (see paragraph 7, "Intelligence, Surveillance, and Reconnaissance Considerations") or strike for the desired effect. Depending on the desired effect, there may be more than one type of asset available to support a particular requirement. UASs are typically high demand assets due to mission duration, the ability to quickly respond to dynamic requests, and their ability to support multiple users. There are three categories of UAS tasking: preplanned, immediate, and dynamic.

1. **Preplanned.** UASs tasked by the JFACC. Requests for direct support of a preplanned mission should be requested using the forms and procedures established for the theater, such as Department of Defense Form 1972, Joint Tactical Air Strike Request, or the Air Support Request.

2. **Immediate.** Requests are submitted outside the ATO cycle and expedited through internet relay chat, email, telephone, or radio, as required. Immediate requests are sent directly to the JAOC.

3. **Dynamic.** Redirects UASs from an existing mission to a new target based on published priorities and criteria. Historically, reasons for retasking include troops in contact, high priority target opportunities, and PR. Procedures for dynamic retasking of UAS assets in-flight to meet an immediate UAS support request are governed by the OPLAN, ROE, and/or SPINS.

(b) **Retasking a UAS** must be carefully considered. Dynamic retasking of a UAS should be done by the governing C2 agency and only after evaluating the full impact of diverting the capability from the current mission and the impact to operational success or consequences without the asset. PED, which includes specific, well-defined essential elements of information and reporting instructions, must be considered and coordinated when dynamically retasking UASs.

(2) **Transfer of Control During Mission Execution.** If a UAS or the payload is reallocated to support another commander's objective, the supported commander should, to the maximum extent feasible, take advantage of the established C2 architecture. This will alleviate the necessity for the supported commander to understand how assets or payloads, not under the commander's command, are controlled (as opposed to how they can be used). If it is necessary to control an asset by anyone other than the primary UAS operator (e.g., the supported commander wants to control which way to direct an electro-optical infrared camera), then they should be familiar with joint terminology for controlling the UAS and payload.

(3) **UAS C2 for Dynamic Targeting.** Recent operations have demonstrated that UASs can be critical to the success of dynamic targeting missions and prosecution of targets of opportunity (unplanned, unanticipated) or TSTs. UAS controlling agencies should follow established procedures for executing dynamic targeting operations. Dynamic targeting situations may require UASs to support CAS, strike coordination and reconnaissance, air interdictions, other joint fires missions, and PR. Specific tasks for the UASs may include: target acquisition/marking, terminal guidance of ordnance, providing precision coordinates for GPS-aided munitions, delivery of onboard precision-guided ordnance, tactical assessment, BDA, and retargeting (i.e., "shoot-look-shoot"). In the dynamic targeting role, UASs are routed, controlled, and deconflicted in the same manner as tiltrotor, fixed-wing, and rotary-winged manned aircraft, as outlined in joint doctrine.

e. **Counter-UAS.** Adversaries are also developing and acquiring UASs some of which are similar and/or identical to friendly UASs. **It is imperative C2 and DCA nodes are able to differentiate between friendly and enemy UA.** UAS operators must follow prescribed airspace control and air defense identification procedures closely to help prevent friendly fire and/or enemy UAS exploitation of that airspace. Adversaries may attempt to exploit airspace "gaps," so these should be kept to a minimum when developing ACPs. Positive control of airspace is generally most effective for airspace control and air defense, but many smaller UASs are not capable of positive control. The use of coordinating altitudes and other ACMs should be employed for efficient and timely use of the airspace, and to aid air defense operators differentiate between friend and foe UA. Restricted operations zone (ROZ) should be used as an integration tool, not as a segregation tool. When a ROZ is used for other than its intended purpose (as a "space holder," for example), it becomes an inefficient use of airspace that complicates the ACA duties and the air defense mission.

For further details on airspace control procedures, refer to JP 3-52, Joint Airspace Control.

For a more detailed discussion of UAS considerations, see Field Manual (FM) 3-04.15/Marine Corps Reference Publication (MCRP) 3-42.1A/Navy Tactics, Techniques, and Procedures (NTTP) 3-55.14/Air Force Tactics, Techniques, and Procedures (AFTTP) 3-2.64, Multi-Service Tactics, Techniques, and Procedures for Unmanned Aircraft Systems.

10. Personnel Recovery Considerations

Since PR often relies on air assets to accomplish some of the PR execution tasks, coordination between the joint personnel recovery center (JPRC) and JAOC is essential. The JPRC is responsible for providing the information that goes into the PR portion of the ATO SPINS. The JFACC should ensure the ATO includes air assets sufficient to accomplish PR tasks. Deconfliction of PR missions from other air missions is accomplished through the ATO. If the JPRC is not collocated and integrated into the JAOC, it is essential the JPRC director establish a liaison element within the JAOC to facilitate tasking of dedicated PR assets in the ATO, coordinate tasking or redirection of air assets to support PR mission execution, monitor ATO and PR mission execution, coordinate changes to PR information in the ATO SPINS, assess the effectiveness of PR, and recommend changes to JFC/JFACC guidance for PR. Service components should establish a personnel recovery coordination cell (PRCC)/rescue coordination team (RCT) to coordinate all component PR activities. When the JFACC is the supported commander for PR, the PRCC/RCT and associated communications structure may be collocated and form the nucleus of the JPRC. In this case, the PRCC/RCT, when augmented by other members of the joint force, is normally designated as the JPRC and the JPRC director is tasked with coordinating all PR joint activities. Coordination of PR missions, employing JFACC assets, requires integration with the J-3 and COD. The details for PR can usually be found in annex C, appendix 5 of the JAOP.

For additional information on joint PR, see JP 3-50, Personnel Recovery.

11. Chemical, Biological, Radiological, and Nuclear Environments

Air operations planning, C2, and mission execution are all impacted by the potential for chemical, biological, radiological, and nuclear (CBRN) hazards (produced by enemy, friendly or neutral actions) on the surface or at multiple levels within the air domain.

Planning should identify, assess, and estimate the adversary's CBRN capabilities, intentions, and most likely COAs, and provide recommendations to senior commanders to protect against, counter, and/or mitigate their effects. Options for generating and executing missions in a CBRN environment, to include issues for airspace control, must be assessed. Intelligence collection missions may be more likely to encounter CBRN hazards, and in some cases, will be the objective of the intelligence collection mission to locate and characterize CBRN threats and hazards. As such, taskings should consider specific platform CBRN contamination avoidance or CBRN hazard survivability capabilities/limitations.

For more detailed information on operations in a CBRN environment, see JP 3-11, Operations in Chemical, Biological, Radiological, and Nuclear Environments.

12. Operations Near International Borders

Near border operations are particularly difficult because the violation of a border can become a major incident complicating the integrity of an operation. Near border operations require close coordination between Services, multinational partners, the ACA, and more. Near border operations must be closely coordinated by the Services, JFACC, other component commanders, and multinational partners. Staffs including public affairs and the staff judge advocate must be prepared to deal effectively with the anticipated and other outcomes of near border operations.

13. Command and Control of Space Forces

a. Commander, USSTRATCOM normally retains OPCON and TACON of assigned space forces, even if they are deployed within the AOR of a GCC. Space forces typically operate in general or direct support to other JFCs. Supported commanders identify priorities to ensure there is clear guidance on the supported commander's intent, integrate space capabilities into planning and operations, and consider the impact if space capabilities are unavailable. GCCs may designate a SCA and delegate appropriate authorities for planning and integrating space requirements and support for the theater.

b. If the desired effects produced by space operations are focused primarily on a single theater, transfer of space forces to a GCC may be appropriate. In this case, forces may be transferred OPCON and/or TACON as appropriate, depending on the ability of the theater commander to command and control space operations, as well as other factors like the nature and duration of the operation and the degree of integration (particularly timing and tempo) with non-space assets that is required.

For more information on the C2 of space forces, see JP 3-14, Space Operations.

14. Air Operations in Maritime Surface Warfare

Air operations in maritime surface warfare are missions involving air assets conducting maritime surface warfare. Seamless integration of joint air assets conducting maritime surface warfare enables effective joint and multinational air participation to plan and execute six specific missions: surface surveillance coordination, armed reconnaissance/strike coordination and reconnaissance, war-at-sea strike, counter fast attack craft/fast inshore attack craft, surface combat air patrol, and airborne maritime mining.

For more information, refer to MCRP 3-25J, NTTP 3-20.8, AFTTP 3-2.74, Air Operations in Maritime Surface Warfare.

APPENDIX A
SAMPLE MISSION STATEMENT AND COMMANDER'S INTENT

The initiation or mission analysis stages of the JOPPA should produce a mission statement and a statement of the commander's intent, both approved by the JFACC.

Sample Mission Statement

"When directed, JFACC-West conducts joint air operations in the Pacific region to protect the deployment of the joint force and to deter aggression.

Should deterrence fail, JFACC-West, on order, gains air superiority in order to enable multinational military operations within the operational area. Concurrently, JFACC-West supports JFLCC-West in order to prevent seizure of NV Pacifica mineral fields.

On order, JFACC-West shapes the operational environment for a joint counteroffensive, supports JFMCC-West for maritime superiority and JFLCC-West for ground offensive operations, degrades conventional military power, and destroys WMD long/medium delivery capability in order to defeat the military forces in the region."

Sample Statement of Commander's Intent:

Purpose. The purpose of the joint air operation is to deter aggression. Should deterrence fail, I will gain and maintain air superiority, conduct joint offensive air operations, and support the JFLCC counteroffensive in order to restore the territorial integrity and ensure the establishment of a legitimate government in a stable Pacifica region.

Military End-State. At the end of this operation:

a. Adversary military forces will be capable of limited defensive operations, have ceased offensive combat operations, and complied with multinational war termination conditions.

b. Adversary will retain no WMD capability.

c. Allied territorial integrity will be restored.

d. JFACC-West will have passed ATC to local authorities.

e. JFACC-West will have been disestablished.

Intentionally Blank

APPENDIX B
JOINT AIR ESTIMATE OF THE SITUATION TEMPLATE

1. Introduction

The JFACC's estimate of the situation is often produced as the culmination of the air COA development and selection stages of the JOPPA. It can be submitted in response to or in support of creation of a JFC's estimate of the situation. It should also be used to assist in creation of the JAOP and daily AODs (as required). It reflects the JFACC's analysis of the various air COAs that may be used to accomplish the assigned mission(s) and contains the recommendation for the best air COA. The estimate may contain as much supporting detail as needed to assist further plan development, but if the air estimate is submitted to the JFC or CCDR for a COA decision, it will generally be submitted in greatly abbreviated format, providing only the information essential to the JFC for arriving at a decision. The following is a **notional** example of a joint air estimate in paragraph format. Use of the format is desirable, but not mandatory and may be abbreviated or elaborated where appropriate. It is often published in message format.

For additional information on commander's estimates, see Chairman of the Joint Chiefs of Staff Manual (CJCSM) 3122.01, Joint Operation Planning and Execution System (JOPES) Volume I, Planning Policies and Procedures, *and CJCSM 3130.03,* Adaptive Planning and Execution (APEX) Planning Guidance and Formats.

2. Joint Air Estimate of the Situation Template

a. **Mission.** State the assigned or deduced mission and its purpose.

(1) JFC's mission statement (from the JFC's estimate) or other overarching guidance if the latter is unavailable.

(2) JFACC's mission statement. Include additional language indicating how overarching guidance will be supported, as required.

b. **Situation and Courses of Action**

(1) Commanders' Intent:

(a) JFC's intent statement, if available (or other overarching guidance stipulating the end state, as required).

(b) JFACC's intent statement (see Appendix A, "Sample Mission Statement and Commander's Intent").

(2) Objectives. Explicitly state air component objectives and the effects required to support their achievement. Include as much detail as required to ensure that each objective is clear, decisive, attainable, and measurable.

(3) Summary of the Results of JIPOE. Include a brief summary of the major factors pertaining to the characteristics of the operating environment and the relative capabilities of all actors within it that may have a significant impact on alternative air COAs.

(4) Adversary Capability. Highlight, if applicable, the adversary capabilities and psychological characteristics that can seriously affect the accomplishment of the mission, giving information that would be useful in evaluating the various air COAs. This section should describe, at a minimum, the enemy's most likely and most dangerous potential COAs.

(5) Force Protection Requirements. Describe potential threats to friendly forces, including such things as the threat of terrorist action prior to, during, and after the mission that can significantly affect accomplishment of the mission.

(6) Own Courses of Action. List air COAs that offer suitable, feasible, and acceptable means of accomplishing the mission. If specific air COAs were prescribed in the WARNING ORDER, they must be included. For each air COA, the following specific information should be addressed:

(a) Combat Forces Required. List capabilities needed, and, if applicable, specific units or platforms. For each, list the following, if known:

1. Force provider.

2. Destination.

3. Required delivery date(s).

4. Coordinated deployment estimate.

5. Employment estimate.

6. Strategic lift requirements, if appropriate.

(b) ISR Forces Required. List capabilities needed, and, if applicable, specific units or capabilities.

(c) PR Capabilities Required. List capabilities needed, and, if applicable, specific units or organizational capabilities.

(d) Support Forces Required. List capabilities needed, and, if applicable, specific units or capabilities.

c. **Analysis of Opposing Courses of Action.** Highlight adversary capabilities and intent (where known) that may have significant impact on friendly COAs.

d. **Comparison of Own Courses of Action.** For submission to the JFC, include only the final statement of conclusions and provide a brief rationale for the favored air COA.

Discuss the relative advantages and disadvantages of the alternative air COAs if this **will assist the JFC in arriving at a decision.**

    e. **Recommended COA.** State the JFACC's recommended COA.

Intentionally Blank

APPENDIX C
JOINT AIR OPERATIONS PLAN TEMPLATE

The JAOP format generally follows the same format as the JFC's OPLAN but from an air power point of view. Each air operations plan will differ with the JOA, situation, and capabilities of the joint force. A sample template follows:

Copy No.
Issuing Headquarters
Place of Issue
Date/Time Group of Signature

JOINT AIR OPERATIONS PLAN:
(Number or Code Name)

REFERENCES: Relevant documents, maps, and charts. This should generally include CJCSM 3130.03, *Adaptive Planning and Execution (APEX) Planning Formats and Guidance*.

1. SITUATION

Briefly describe the situation that the plan addresses (see the JFC's estimate and the following template as a guide). Related OPLAN(s) should be identified, as appropriate.

a. **General Guidance.** Summarize the operational environment and overall JFC mission, guidance, intent, prioritized effects, operational limitations, and specified tasks for the JFACC and established support relationships among components that are relevant to that guidance.

b. **Area of Concern.** Description of and applicable boundaries of the operational area(s), area(s) of interest, etc. Include maps as appropriate.

c. **Deterrent Options.** Describe air power's role in these JFC options, if applicable.

d. **Adversary Forces**. Overview of the hostile threat, to include:

(1) Composition, location, disposition, and movement of major adversary forces and capabilities that can influence action in the operational environment.

(2) Adversary strategic concept (if known): should include adversary's perception of friendly vulnerabilities and adversary's intention regarding those vulnerabilities.

(3) Major adversary objectives (strategic and operational).

(4) Adversary commanders' motivations, thought patterns, idiosyncrasies, and doctrinal patterns (to the extent known).

(5) Operational and sustained capabilities (all relevant adversary forces, not just air and counterair).

(6) Adversary COGs and decisive points.

(a) Analysis of CCs, critical requirements (CRs), and CVs for each.

(b) Description using LOOs and LOEs, if appropriate.

e. **Friendly Forces.** Overview of friendly (US and multinational partner), to include:

(1) Forces available according to TPFDD considerations.

(2) Forces required, based on employment CONOPS. Highlight shortfalls.

(3) Intent of higher, adjacent, and supporting US and multinational forces and commands.

(4) Friendly COGs.

(a) Analysis of CCs, CRs, and CVs.

(b) Steps to be taken to protect friendly CVs.

f. **Assumptions.** List, as required.

g. **Legal Considerations.** List those of critical importance to operations, such as legal restrictions and guidance on targeting. Refer to Annexes, as required.

2. **MISSION**

JFACC's Mission Statement

3. **EXECUTION**

a. **CONOPS for Joint Air Operations.** A statement of the JFACC's intent, objectives, desired effects, and broad employment concepts, to include LOOs and LOEs for the desired end state. Phase plans for each phase of the operation.

(1) Operational concept for the phase, including objectives (ongoing and specific to the phase), intent, desired effects, risk, LOOs, LOEs, plan of operations, timing, and duration.

(2) General guidance for subordinate units and component's supported and supporting requirements. Ensure that all subordinates' missions are complementary.

(3) Forces or capabilities required by objective.

(4) "Be prepared to" missions; phase branches.

(5) Reserve capabilities and/or forces, if applicable–reserve in this sense meaning capabilities held in operational reserve, not Reserve Component elements of the joint force.

(6) Mobility considerations, such as transportation, lines of communications, overflight, and basing that are unique to the phase of the operation.

(7) Information-related capabilities that contribute to IO, such as military deception, military information support operations, and operations security that are unique to the phase of the operation.

(8) Cyberspace operations considerations, such as DOD information-related operations, offensive cyberspace operations, and defensive cyberspace operations that are unique to the phase.

b. **Tasks.** State the component's supporting and supported requirements for the operation in general. Include implied tasks and guidance to subordinates that are not specific to a given phase of the operation.

c. **Coordinating Instructions.** Explain operational terms required for complete understanding of the operation, but which are not defined in current JPs.

d. **Exchange of LNOs.** Explain and direct any liaison requirements here, including the role of the JACCE.

4. ADMINISTRATION AND LOGISTICS

a. **Concept of Sustainment.** A broad statement of the functional areas of logistics, transportation, personnel policies, and administration, if required.

b. **Logistics.** Broad sustainment concept for air operations. Phase considerations (synchronized with execution phases–may not be required if already explained in phase plans).

(1) Basing and Overflight. Explain any unique clearance and buildup requirements in this section, if not already explained in phase plans.

(2) Lines of Communications. Explain any requirements relevant to the operation.

(3) Base Opening and Development. Explain any general base opening requirements for the operation. Information may also be included in phase plans.

(4) Maintenance and Modification. Use as required.

(5) Host Nation Considerations. Explain any unique requirements for the operation.

(6) Reconstitution of Forces. Use as required.

(7) Inter-Service, Interagency, and Inter-Component Requirements. Use as required.

(8) Foreign Military Assistance. Use as required.

c. **Personnel.** Use as required.

d. **Public Affairs.** Identify key public affairs requirements necessitated by major event (may also be identified in phase plans).

e. **Civil Affairs.** Use as required.

f. **Meteorological and Oceanographic.** Explain factors like climate and terrain, and how they will likely affect air operations.

g. **Geospatial Information.** Explain common geospatial reference system requirements and plans here.

h. **Medical Services.** Use as required.

5. COMMAND AND CONTROL

a. **Command**

(1) Command Relationships. Specify command relationships for all organizations relevant to the JFACC operations. Be as specific as possible.

(2) Memoranda of Understanding. As applicable.

(3) Command Headquarters. Designation and location of all air-capable command headquarters.

(4) Continuity of Operations. Any general considerations unique to the operation.

(5) Command Posts. List the designations and locations of each major headquarters.

(6) Succession to Command. Designate, in order of succession, the commanders responsible for assuming command of the operation in specific applicable circumstances.

b. **C2 and Communications Systems.** General overview of C2 systems and communication systems required to support air operations.

6. ANNEXES

JAOP annexes should be written for a functional domain-specific audience and contain technical details necessary for C2 of all air organizations and capabilities across the joint force. They should contain any details not considered appropriate for the relevant section of the main plan.

A. **Task Organization.**

B. **Intelligence.**

C. **Operations.**

D. **Logistics.**

E. **Personnel.**

F. **Public Affairs.**

G. **Civil Affairs.**

H. **Meteorological and Oceanographic Operations.**

I. **Force Protection**

J. **Command Relationships.**

K. **Joint Communications System.**

L. **Environmental Considerations.**

M. **Geospatial Information and Services.**

N. **Space Operations.**

P. **Host-Nation Support.**

Q. **Medical Services.**

S. **Special Technical Operations.**

V. **Interagency Coordination.**

(Signed) (Commander)

DISTRIBUTION:
SECURITY CLASSIFICATION.

Intentionally Blank

APPENDIX D
AIR OPERATIONS DIRECTIVE TEMPLATE

Issuing Headquarters
Place of Issue
AOD Effective Period
Date/Time Group of Signature

1. SITUATION

    a. JFC guidance (verbatim).

        (1) JFC's intent statement.

        (2) Execution guidance (if issued).

        (3) Supported and supporting command relationships.

    b. Enemy situation.

    c. Friendly situation (by joint force component).

2. MISSION

The JFACC's mission statement (verbatim). Covers all phases of the operation, but AOD may state which phase this AOD applies to. This should not change unless the mission itself changes.

3. EXECUTION–AIR OPERATIONS

    a. JFACC's intent.

        (1) Purpose.

        (2) End state.

    b. Execution: What to do, when.

    c. Focus of effort by objective.

    d. Weight of effort by objective.

    e. Acceptable level of risk.

    f. Collateral damage and civilian casualty guidance.

    g. TST guidance.

    h. Other issues (e.g., ISR, IO, space, mobility, focus of effort, PR).

4. ADMINISTRATION AND LOGISTICS

Logistics considerations affecting operations during the AOD period.

5. COMMAND AND CONTROL

C2 considerations affecting operations during the AOD period. If there are no unique considerations, refer the reader to the JAOP commander relationship annex.

6. ANNEXES

Use as required. Typical annexes:

a. Full listing of end state conditions, objectives, effects, and tasks, including MOP and effectiveness for each (as applicable).

b. Commander's critical information requirements and essential elements of information applicable for the AOD period.

APPENDIX E
JOINT AIR OPERATIONS CENTER DIVISIONS AND DESCRIPTIONS

1. Joint Air Operations Center Director

The JAOC director is charged with effectively managing joint air operations and establishing the JAOC battle rhythm. The JAOC director develops and directs processes to plan, coordinate, allocate, task, execute, and assess joint air operations in the JOA based on JFC and JFACC guidance. The JAOC director's staff includes division chiefs, ATO coordinators, the JAOC manager, information management personnel, and the ATO SPINS coordinator (see Figure E-1).

2. Strategy Division

The SD concentrates on long-range and near-term planning of joint air operations to achieve JFC objectives by developing, refining, disseminating, and assessing the JFACC's strategy. In addition, the SD does near-term planning for space, cyberspace, and IO in coordination with joint air operations. Strategy activities are primarily reflected in the JAOP, AOD, and the operational assessment report. The SD is divided into four teams: strategy plans, strategy guidance, IO, and operational assessment. Despite physical proximity to the ATO planning, production, and execution areas within the JAOC, SD personnel should not become caught up in execution details. Although the IO team is organizationally aligned with the SD, it coordinates IO efforts across all the divisions within the JAOC.

3. Combat Plans Division

The CPD is responsible for near-term air operations planning (within 48 hours prior to ATO execution). The CPD is divided into four teams: TET, MAAP, ATO production, and C2 plans. The TET develops the JFACC's TNL and may produce a draft JIPTL for JFC approval. The primary daily products of CPD processes are the ATO and ACO. CPD develops the MAAP, assembles the SPINS, and ISR synchronization matrix. The MAAP team needs the current AOD, ABP shell, preplanned AIRSUPREQs and JIPTL loaded to build missions in the proper TBMCS format. The C2 plans team produces the daily ACO, tactical operations data, and operational task link message. The ATO production team develops the ABP databases, and assembles, publishes, and disseminates the ATO and SPINS. Additionally, various specialty/support personnel are embedded in the CPD.

4. Combat Operations Division

The COD is responsible for the execution of the current ATO (usually the 24 hours encompassing the effective period of the ATO). The COD is divided into four teams: offensive operations, defensive operations, interface control, and the senior intelligence duty officer (SIDO) team. Additionally, various specialty/support personnel are embedded in the COD.

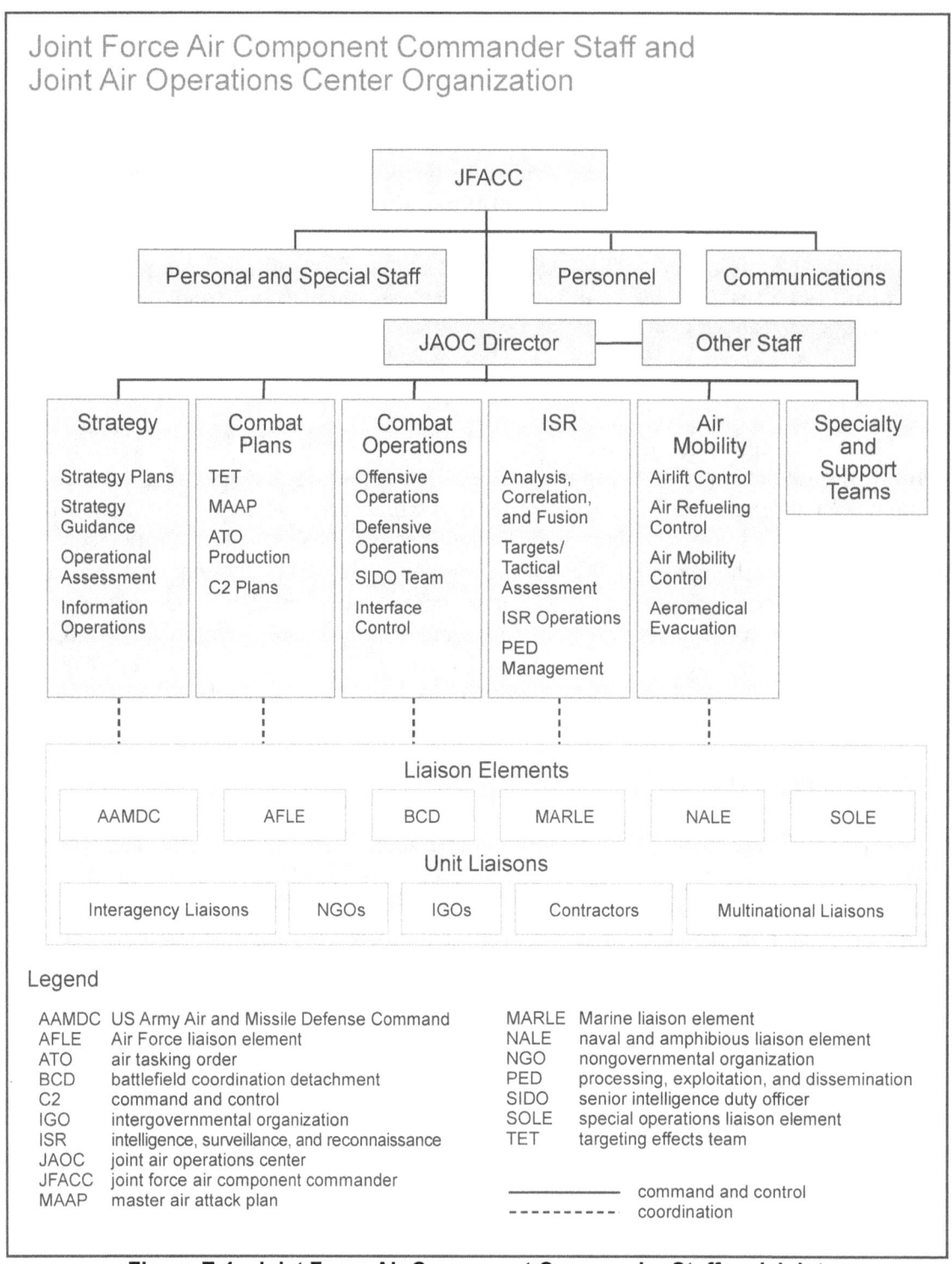

**Figure E-1. Joint Force Air Component Commander Staff and Joint
Air Operations Center Organization**

5. Intelligence, Surveillance, and Reconnaissance Division

For operations in theaters outside the continental United States, the ISRD is responsible for providing the JFACC and JAOC with awareness of adversary activity in the operational area, assisting with integrating, planning, and managing airborne ISR operations, developing and maintaining targeting information about the adversary, and assisting with execution of ISR operations. In addition, ISRD has integrated teams or assigned personnel in other JAOC divisions. The ISRD is divided into four teams: analysis, correlation and fusion; targets and tactical assessment; ISR operations; and PED team. ISR personnel, assigned in the SD, assist in the development of overall JFACC strategy, JAOP and operational assessment. ISR personnel, assigned in the CPD, provide tailored ISR operations planning, threat analysis, and targeting expertise necessary to develop detailed execution plans for joint air operations. ISR personnel, assigned to the COD, are part of the SIDO team and provide current situational awareness, targeting, and ISR operations management for execution of the ATO.

6. Air Mobility Division

The AMD plans, coordinates, tasks, and executes the air mobility mission in support of the joint air planning and execution process. The AMD consists of four teams: airlift control team (ALCT), air refueling control team (ARCT), air mobility control team (AMCT), and aeromedical evacuation control team (AECT). ALCT plans, schedules, and tasks the theater airlift portion of the ATO. The ARCT plans, schedules, tasks, and assists in execution of air refueling missions. The AMCT manages the execution of the air mobility missions in the ATO and provides support for the overall air mobility effort. The AECT plans, schedules, and monitors execution of AE missions and AE assets to support patient movements. Elements within the AMD are matrixed throughout other divisions.

7. Specialty and Support Functions

Various specialty and support teams provide the JAOC with diverse capabilities to help integrate and orchestrate joint air operations. Examples of these functions include force protection, public affairs, PR, staff judge advocate, weather, airspace management, and information management. Integration of specialty and support capabilities is crucial to the success of the JAOC and joint air operations.

Intentionally Blank

APPENDIX F
LIAISON ELEMENTS WITHIN THE JOINT AIR OPERATIONS CENTER

1. Introduction

Liaison between forces is essential for coordinated and effective joint air operations. Component commanders will exchange liaison elements to assist and coordinate the planning and execution of their component's operations with joint air operations. Liaison elements provide senior-level interface for air, land, maritime, and SOF. These elements consist of personnel who provide component planning and tasking expertise, coordination capabilities, and the ability to deconflict component operations and joint air operations. A brief summary follows of typical liaison elements. Detailed information can be found in respective command and Service documents.

2. Battlefield Coordination Detachment

The Army Service component commander provides the BCD as a liaison element to the Service component commander designated as the JFACC or to the Air Force Service component if a JFACC is not designated. The BCD facilitates the synchronization of air and Army ground operations within the operational area. It expedites information exchange through face-to-face coordination with JAOC division/teams because the BCD personnel are trained to operate in the JAOC environment using both Army systems and joint air C2 systems, and understand the operations process, joint C2 processes (e.g., joint targeting) and the air component processes (e.g., joint air tasking cycle). The BCD coordinates and receives objectives, guidance, and priorities from the ARFOR commander and staff. Specific missions include processing, monitoring and interpreting the land battle situation, providing the necessary interface for the exchange of current intelligence and operational data, coordinating air and missile defense, and airspace coordination. Additionally, the BCD supervises the Army air reconnaissance liaison teams and Army ground liaison detachments that coordinate ARFOR requirements with supporting Air Force reconnaissance, fighter, and airlift wings. BCD personnel work with their counterparts in the JAOC to facilitate planning, coordination, and execution of air-ground operations by ensuring that:

a. The JFACC understands the Army commander's operational intent, priorities, objectives, and air support requirements.

b. Pertinent Army command operational data and operational support requirements are forwarded to the JFACC to include AIRSUPREQs, airspace control means requests, manned and unmanned information collection, cyberspace and electromagnetic activities, airlift, and joint suppression of enemy air defenses.

c. Army requests for airspace coordination and air support are coordinated with the appropriate elements.

d. The ATO accurately reflects air support to the Army and Army aircraft missions, and the ACO reflects ACMs approved for the Army.

e. All changes to theater-wide air defense warnings, weapons control status, ROEs, and aircraft identification standards among the JAOC, Army force headquarters, and senior land-based air and missile defense headquarters are coordinated.

f. Planned and unplanned changes to the fire support coordination line and selected fire support coordination measures are coordinated as required.

g. Army airspace risk guidance and airspace use priorities are coordinated with the appropriate joint C2 elements/JAOC.

h. Priorities of JFC airspace risk guidance and airspace use are forwarded to the senior Army headquarters.

i. Priorities for use of joint air assets and changes to missions supporting ground forces are forwarded to the senior Army headquarters.

3. Special Operations Liaison Element

The JFSOCC provides a SOLE to the JFACC, or appropriate Service component air C2 facility, to coordinate and synchronize SOF, air and surface operations with joint air operations. The SOLE director places LNOs throughout the JFACC's staff, located in the JAOC. The SOLE coordinates, synchronizes, and deconflicts all SOF air, surface, and subsurface activities by providing a SOF presence in the JAOC that is aware of the activities of special operations units in the field. Special operations must be closely coordinated with joint air operations planning and execution to prevent friendly fire, and ensure achievement of mission objectives.

For more information on the SOLE, see JP 3-05, Special Operations; *and United States Special Operations Command (USSOCOM) Directive 525-7,* Joint Special Operations Liaison Element.

4. Naval and Amphibious Liaison Element

The JFMCC/NCC should establish a NALE to coordinate with the JAOC on matters pertaining to Navy and Marine amphibious, maritime, and air operations, and to serve as the MOC's primary point of contact in the AOC. Placement of billets at the JAOC will be in coordination with the appropriate commanders' guidance (JFACC and JFMCC/NCC) and should facilitate synchronization of maneuver and synergy of effects. The NALE integrates JFMCC objectives into the AOD, advocates JFMCC/NCC target nominations to reflect desired effects in the JFC's JIPTL, and coordinates, integrates, and deconflicts all naval air and surface activities in the JFACC's ATO and ACO. The NALE facilitates JFMCC requests for air support, and monitors and interprets the maritime battle situation for the JAOC. The NALE supports incorporation of naval assets into the ATO, ensuring JFMCC/NCC assets are suitably integrated into joint air operations. The NALE provides the necessary interface for the exchange of current operational and intelligence data between the components and the JAOC. The NALE also coordinates maritime requirements for air defense support, long-range interdiction, and monitors maritime airspace and ATC requirements and changes within the maritime AO or AOA, as specified. The NALE provides feedback to the JAOC and components on current and future joint air operations concerning integration of force requirements. Specialty/platform LNO positions may be required to be in the JAOC to cover specific maritime platforms and capabilities that require special coordination.

5. Marine Liaison Element

The MARLE is the Marine Corps forces commander's representative within the JAOC and is responsive to the JFACC on matters pertaining to Marine Corps operations. The MARLE provides feedback to organizations within the JAOC on current and future joint air operations concerning integration of force requirements.

6. Air Force Liaison Element

The AFLE provides an interface between the COMAFFOR and the JFACC for coordinating and synchronizing Air Force units in support of joint air operations if the JFACC is not also the COMAFFOR. Normally, the AFLE is composed of personnel and equipment for a general purpose, numbered Air Force's staff and component organizations. AFLE manning is based on a cadre concept with personnel selected for their battle management expertise and knowledge of C2 concepts and procedures. The cadres are augmented by additional personnel who are specialists knowledgeable in the capabilities and tactics of the aircraft, intelligence, or weapons systems being employed. The AFLE can be tailored to perform a variety of missions and management functions to match the contingency or operation.

7. Army Air and Missile Defense Command Liaison Team

The AAMDC liaison team is the senior Army and air defense element. It is the primary interface for all land-based Army air and theater missile defense operations. The BCD air defense section will coordinate its activities with the AAMDC liaison if required. Although the BCD has an air defense section, responsibility to integrate the ARFOR air and missile defense resides with the senior air defense artillery commander, normally the commander, AAMDC. The AAMDC liaison team responsibilities normally include:

a. Assisting the AADC with the AADP development.

b. Integrating land-based air and missile defense into theater defensive operations.

c. Advising the JFACC/AADC regarding ROE, ACMs related to air defense, weapons control measures, fire control orders, and air defense warnings.

d. Advising the AADC on matters regarding land-based air and missile defense operations.

8. Other Liaison

Liaisons representing multinational forces or interagency organizations may improve JAOC situational awareness and contribute to unity of effort. They provide invaluable information on their nations' (or agencies') capabilities and sensitivities. They can also help overcome cultural barriers. The JFACC must anticipate the need for LNOs and be prepared to proactively coordinate as appropriate.

See JP 3-0, Joint Operations, *JP 3-08,* Interorganizational Coordination During Joint Operations, *and JP 3-16,* Multinational Operations, *for further discussion on the subject.*

APPENDIX G
THE JOINT AIR COMPONENT COORDINATION ELEMENT

1. General

A JACCE is a small team of airpower experts that can be used to facilitate coordination between a JFACC and other component commanders or the JFC. The JACCE is intended as a facilitator, and should not be used in place of existing, more formal methods of coordination. The JACCE will not bear any responsibilities of the JAOC nor will it replace any JAOC processes or sub-processes. The JFACC may simultaneously deploy multiple JACCEs as liaisons to the JTF, subordinate joint forces, or Services, while operating from home station or a deployed location. Some general considerations include:

a. **The JACCE director** should be senior enough to work effectively with the JFC or component commander whom they are supporting.

b. **The JACCE director should be supported by a staff.** Its size should reflect the breadth of the operation and normally includes plans, operations, intelligence, airspace management, space, and air mobility. Additionally, administration and communications support may be needed.

(1) The JACCE staff should be representative of the JFACC's staff and should be composed primarily of personnel from the JFACC's Service or component (e.g., if the JFACC is a naval officer and the JAOC is composed primarily of naval personnel, then the JACCE should also be composed primarily of naval personnel).

(2) JACCE composition and expertise should be tailored to the needs of the supported/supporting headquarters. For example, the JACCE composition and expertise required for combat operations may be considerably different than those required for a dedicated humanitarian operation.

c. **Authority and responsibility** of the JACCE should be tailored to JFACC needs. In some situations the JFACC may give the JACCE significant latitude in their authority to represent the JFACC; in other cases the JFACC may be more restrictive.

d. **Working Relationships.** The JFACC should introduce the JACCE director to the supported component commander or JFC to establish the desired working relationship. If this is not possible, the JFACC should at least meet face-to-face with the JACCE prior to the JACCE assuming their duties. Typically, when Army units are designated to provide the JTF or JFLCC and the COMAFFOR is designated the JFACC, the habitually aligned air support operations group will provide the JACCE nucleus due to the established working relationships.

e. **Communications.** A key to the JACCE's success is its ability to communicate and gather information. Better communication should lead to better information and thus to better advice from the JACCE. Some members of the JACCE will require access to special access programs or compartmentalized information and they should deploy with the requisite clearances.

2. Presentation and Command and Control Relationships

Ideally, the JFACC and other component commanders would be located together and there would be no need for a JACCE—the JFACC and other commanders could work side-by-side and talk face-to-face. Headquarters are often not located together, however, so a JACCE is presented to the other commanders in order to bridge that physical separation. The JFACC retains OPCON of the JACCE, but Service components retain administrative control of their personnel within it. There are two general modes of JACCE presentation: internal and external to a JTF.

a. Presentation with JFACC internal to a JTF

(1) In this model the CCDR has established a JTF, the JFACC is subordinate to the commander, JTF, and JACCE are presented as needed laterally to other functional component commanders and upward to the JTF. This is illustrated in Figure G-1.

(2) Although a JSOTF normally includes a JSOACC, the JSOACC is focused on employment of SOF aviation. A JACCE may be required if conventional aviation provided by the JFACC is to be integrated with SOF to provide non-SOF capabilities.

b. Presentation with JFACC external to a JTF.
In this model there is a mix of several JTFs within a theater, but only one fully capable JAOC to service all components. In such instances, there is usually one JFACC reporting to the GCC. The JFACC provides centralized control of all joint air power across the theater and supports multiple JTFs based on the CCDR's priorities. This arrangement usually occurs because there are insufficient air assets to supply each JTF with adequate air component representation and thus there is no separate air component within the JTFs.

c. Presentation to Service components.
In those cases when a JFC elects not to designate functional component commanders, the COMAFFOR may provide air component coordination elements to the other Service component commanders and the JFC as necessary. Duties and relationships remain as stated.

Example 1: During Operations Iraqi Freedom and Enduring Freedom, the Commander of United States Air Forces Central Command, while acting as the joint force air component commander for the Commander, United States Central Command, simultaneously provides support to separate JTFs [joint task forces] in Iraq, Afghanistan, and the Horn of Africa.

Example 2: The Commander, United States Air Forces Northern Command, acting as the Joint Force Air Component Commander for Operation NOBLE EAGLE in the CONUS [continental United States], may also support separate JTFs responding to separate disasters in CONUS. In this case, if there are very limited Air Force forces operational control to the JTF, then the JACCE [joint air component coordination element] director could be dual-hatted as the commander, Air Force forces, depending on the JACCE director's ability to handle both jobs.

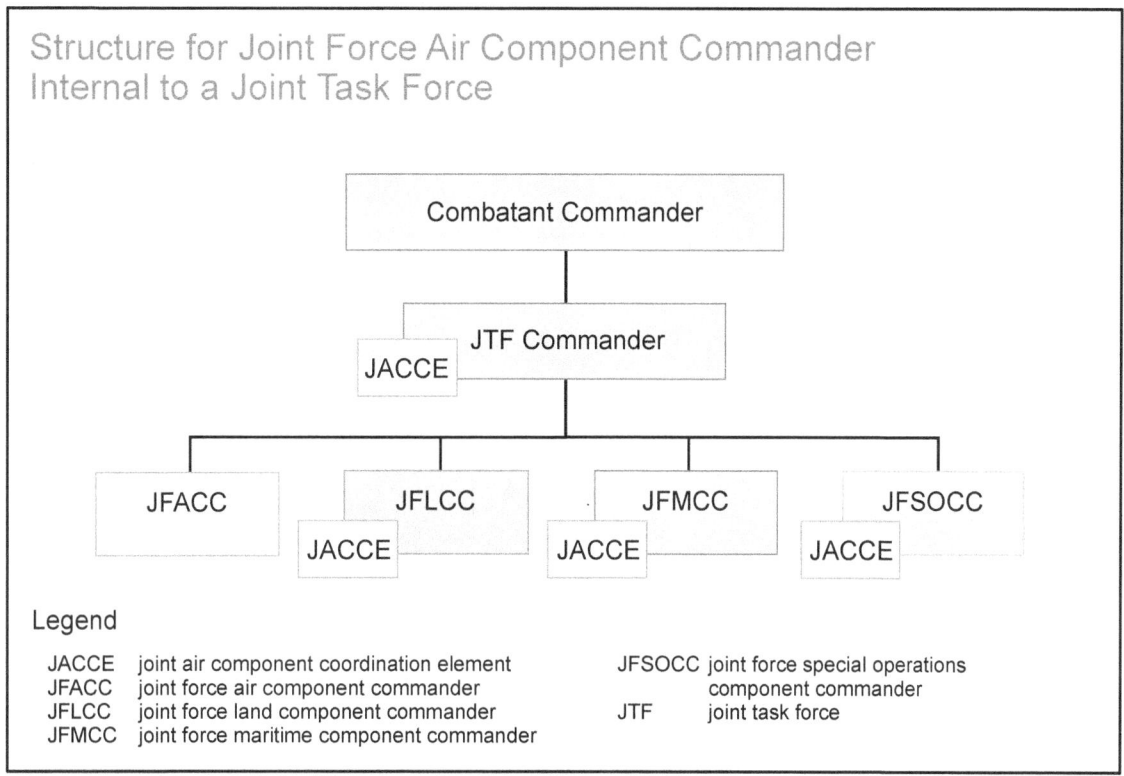

Figure G-1. Structure for Joint Force Air Component Commander Internal to a Joint Task Force

d. **Presentation in multinational operations.** In multinational operations JACCEs may be presented as necessary. The model should be similar to that depicted in Figure G-1 above. (See Figure G-2.)

3. Joint Air Component Coordination Element Authority, Command Relationships, and Functions and Responsibilities

The JACCE:

a. Derives all authority from the JFACC.

b. Authorities can vary and change over time, depending on JFACC objectives, CONOPS, and operational dynamics.

c. Is typically presented in a liaison role (i.e., without command authority) and communicates, facilitates, advises, coordinates, and supports the effective interplay between the JFACC and the host commander(s). However, a Service component may delegate some command authorities of Service forces to the JACCE based on operational requirements and to enhance overall C2 and integration and employment.

d. Communicates:

(1) The host commander's decisions, priorities, interests, and plans to the JFACC.

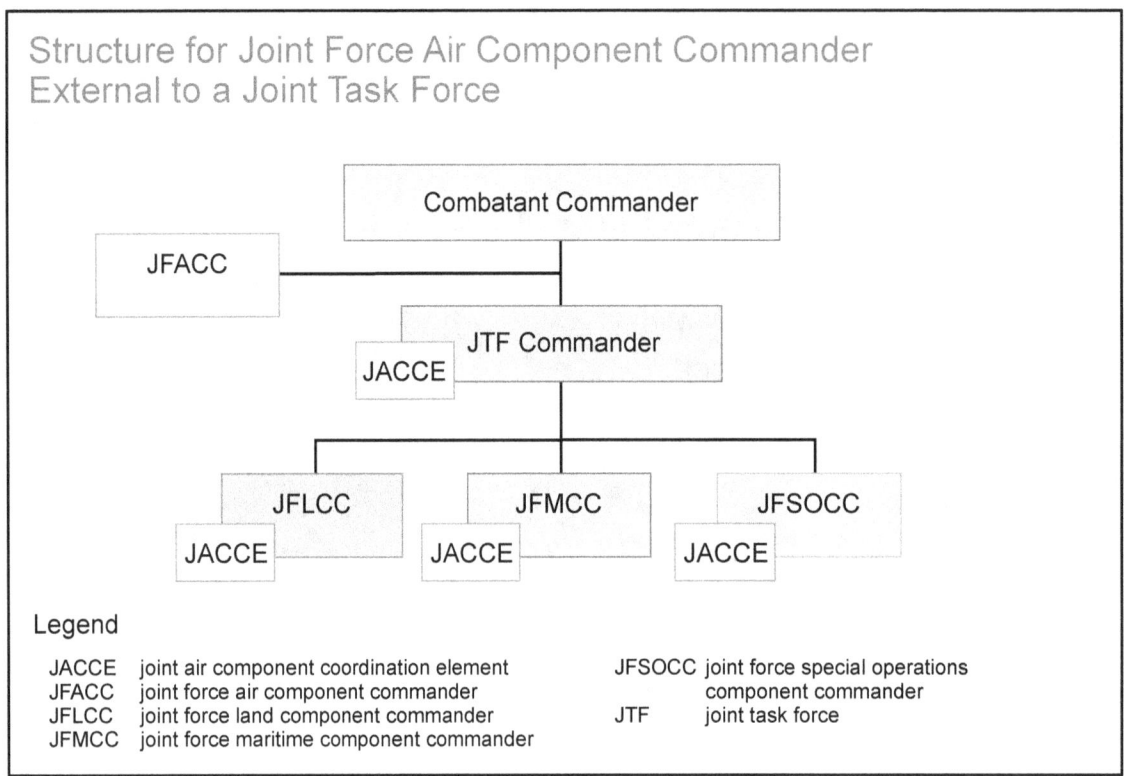

**Figure G-2. Structure for Joint Force Air Component Commander
External to a Joint Task Force**

(2) The JFACC's intent, capabilities, restraints, and air component perspective to the host commander.

e. Advises and assists in planning supporting and supported relationship options.

f. Facilitates the staff process for the JFACC and host commander.

g. Should not replace, replicate, or circumvent in-place request mechanisms (e.g., target requests and air apportionment).

THE JOINT AIR COMPONENT COORDINATION ELEMENT DURING OPERATION IRAQI FREEDOM AND OPERATION ENDURING FREEDOM

In United States Central Command during later operations of Operation IRAQI Freedom and Operation Enduring Freedom, the JFACC [joint force air component commander found the typical liaison role of the ACCE [air component coordination element] [precursor to the joint air component coordination element] insufficient to satisfy his and the supported JFC [joint force commander] requirements. He therefore delegated additional specific responsibilities and personnel, including limited command authority over some forces, to better integrate planning at all levels and respond to JFACC and JFC needs. The ACCE effectively became dual-hatted as an air expeditionary task force commander, which eventually became the final solution.

"To improve the integration of airpower with the ground scheme of maneuver, I empowered the ACCE-Afghanistan and ACCE-Iraq through a verbal order in 2009. Specifically, I delegated limited operational control and full administrative control over AFCENT [United States Air Forces Central] forces in each joint operations area to the respective ACCE.

"Although the tactical control of theater-wide air assets remains at the AFCENT CAOC [Combined Air Operations Center], the ACCE has authority to organize forces, recommend courses of action, and provide authoritative direction to the subordinate air expeditionary wings. The ACCE also ensures that inputs to the air tasking order meet the needs of the operation or plan. Reachback to the Air Force forces staff and the CAOC permits the ACCE to accomplish these tasks without having to maintain a large forward staff and robust command and control capability."

"A Seat at the Table: Beyond the Air Component Coordination Element"
Lt Gen Mike Hostage, US Air Force
Air and Space Power Journal, Winter 2010

Intentionally Blank

APPENDIX H
REFERENCES

The development of JP 3-30 is based upon the following sources:

1. Department of Defense Publications

Department of Defense Directive 5100.01, *Functions of the Department of Defense and Its Major Components*.

2. Chairman of the Joint Chiefs of Staff Publications

a. Chairman of the Joint Chiefs of Staff Instruction 3151.01B, *Global Command and Control System Common Operational Picture Reporting Requirements*.

b. CJCSM 3122.01A, *Joint Operation Planning and Execution System (JOPES), Vol. I, Planning Policies and Procedures*.

c. CJCSM 3130.03, *Adaptive Planning and Execution (APEX) Planning Formats and Guidance*.

d. JP 1, *Doctrine for the Armed Forces of the United States*.

e. JP 2-0, *Joint Intelligence*.

f. JP 2-01, *Joint and National Intelligence Support to Military Operations*.

g. JP 2-01.3, *Joint Intelligence Preparation of the Operational Environment*.

h. JP 3-0, *Joint Operations*.

i. JP 3-01, *Countering Air and Missile Threats*.

j. JP 3-03, *Joint Interdiction*.

k. JP 3-04, *Joint Shipboard Helicopter and Tiltrotor Aircraft Operations*.

l. JP 3-05, *Special Operations*.

m. JP 3-08, *Interorganizational Coordination During Joint Operations*.

n. JP 3-09, *Joint Fire Support*.

o. JP 3-09.3, *Close Air Support*.

p. JP 3-11, *Operations in Chemical, Biological, Radiological, and Nuclear (CBRN) Environments*.

q. JP 3-12, *Cyberspace Operations*.

r. JP 3-13, *Information Operations*.

s. JP 3-13.1, *Electronic Warfare*.

t. JP 3-14, *Space Operations*.

u. JP 3-15.1, *Counter-Improvised Explosive Device Operations*.

v. JP 3-16, *Multinational Operations*.

w. JP 3-17, *Air Mobility Operations*.

x. JP 3-50, *Personnel Recovery*.

y. JP 3-52, *Joint Airspace Control*.

z. JP 3-60, *Joint Targeting*.

aa. JP 4-02, *Health Services*.

bb. JP 5-0, *Joint Operation Planning*.

3. Service Publications

a. Air Force Instruction 13-1 AOC, Volume 3, *Operational Employment Procedures-Air Operations Center (AOC)*.

b. AFTTP 3-3. AOC, *Operational Employment–Air and Space Operations Center*.

c. NTTP 3-03.4, *Naval Strike and Air Warfare*.

d. Army Tactics, Techniques, and Procedures 3-04.15/MCRP 3-42.1A/NTTP 3-55.14/AFTTP(I) 3-2.64, *Multi-Service Tactics, Techniques, and Procedures for Tactical Employment of Unmanned Aircraft Systems*.

e. NTTP 3-20.8/AFTTP 3-2.74, *Multi-Service Tactics, Techniques, and Procedures for Air Operations in Maritime Surface Warfare*.

f. Navy Warfare Publication 3-30, *Naval Command and Control of Air Operations (Organizations and Processes)*.

4. United States Special Operations Command Publications

a. USSOCOM Directive 525-7, *Joint Special Operations Liaison Element*.

b. USSOCOM Directive 525-8, *Joint Special Operations Air Component*.

APPENDIX J
ADMINISTRATIVE INSTRUCTIONS

1. User Comments

Users in the field are highly encouraged to submit comments on this publication to: Joint Staff J-7, Deputy Director, Joint Education and Doctrine Analysis, ATTN: Joint Doctrine Support Division, 116 Lake View Parkway, Suffolk, VA 23435-2697. These comments should address content (accuracy, usefulness, consistency, and organization), writing, and appearance.

2. Authorship

The lead agent for this publication is the US Air Force. The Joint Staff doctrine sponsor for this publication is the J-3.

3. Supersession

This publication supersedes JP 3-30, 12 January 2010, *Command and Control for Joint Air Operations*.

4. Change Recommendations

a. Recommendations for urgent changes to this publication should be submitted:

    TO: LEMAY CENTER MAXWELL AFB AL//CC//
    INFO: JOINT STAFF WASHINGTON DC//J7-JE&D//

b. Routine changes should be submitted electronically to the Deputy Director, Joint Education and Doctrine, ATTN: Joint Doctrine Analysis Division, 116 Lake View Parkway, Suffolk, VA 23435-2697, and info the lead agent and the Director for Joint Force Development, J-7/JE&D.

c. When a Joint Staff directorate submits a proposal to the Chairman of the Joint Chiefs of Staff that would change source document information reflected in this publication, that directorate will include a proposed change to this publication as an enclosure to its proposal. The Services and other organizations are requested to notify the Joint Staff J-7 when changes to source documents reflected in this publication are initiated.

5. Distribution of Publications

Local reproduction is authorized, and access to unclassified publications is unrestricted. However, access to and reproduction authorization for classified JPs must be IAW DOD Manual 5200.01, Volume 1, *DOD Information Security Program: Overview, Classification, and Declassification,* and DOD Manual 5200.01, Volume 3, *DOD Information Security Program: Protection of Classified Information.*

6. Distribution of Electronic Publications

a. Joint Staff J-7 will not print copies of JPs for distribution. Electronic versions are available on JDEIS at https://jdeis.js.mil (NIPRNET) and http://jdeis.js.smil.mil (SIPRNET), and on the JEL at http://www.dtic.mil/doctrine (NIPRNET).

b. Only approved JPs are releasable outside the combatant commands, Services, and Joint Staff. Release of any classified JP to foreign governments or foreign nationals must be requested through the local embassy (Defense Attaché Office) to DIA, Defense Foreign Liaison/IE-3, 200 MacDill Blvd., Joint Base Anacostia-Bolling, Washington, DC 20340-5100.

c. JEL CD-ROM. Upon request of a joint doctrine development community member, the Joint Staff J-7 will produce and deliver one CD-ROM with current JPs. This JEL CD-ROM will be updated not less than semi-annually and when received can be locally reproduced for use within the combatant commands, Services, and combat support agencies.

GLOSSARY
PART I—ABBREVIATIONS AND ACRONYMS

AADC	area air defense commander
AADP	area air defense plan
AAGS	Army air-ground system
AAMDC	United States Army Air and Missile Defense Command
ABP	air battle plan
ACA	airspace control authority
ACE	aviation combat element (USMC)
ACM	airspace coordinating measure
ACO	airspace control order
ACP	airspace control plan
ACS	airspace control system
ADAM	air defense airspace management
AE	aeromedical evacuation
AECT	aeromedical evacuation control team
AETF	air expeditionary task force
AFLE	Air Force liaison element
AFTTP	Air Force tactics, techniques, and procedures
AIRSUPREQ	air support request
ALCT	airlift control team
ALLOREQ	allocation request
AMCT	air mobility control team
AMD	air mobility division
AO	area of operations
AOA	amphibious objective area
AOC	air operations center
AOD	air operations directive
AODB	air operations database
AOR	area of responsibility
ARCT	air refueling control team
ARFOR	Army forces
ASOC	air support operations center
ATC	air traffic control
ATO	air tasking order
AWACS	Airborne Warning and Control System
BAE	brigade aviation element
BCD	battlefield coordination detachment
BDA	battle damage assessment
C2	command and control
CAS	close air support
CBRN	chemical, biological, radiological, and nuclear
CC	critical capability

CCDR	combatant commander
CDRJSOTF	commander, joint special operations task force
CJCSM	Chairman of the Joint Chiefs of Staff manual
CMA	collection management authority
COA	course of action
COD	combat operations division
COG	center of gravity
COMAFFOR	commander, Air Force forces
CONOPS	concept of operations
CPD	combat plans division
CR	critical requirement
CRC	control and reporting center
CV	critical vulnerability
CWC	composite warfare commander
DAL	defended asset list
DASC	direct air support center
DCA	defensive counterair
DHS	Department of Homeland Security
DIRMOBFOR	director of mobility forces
DOD	Department of Defense
DSCA	defense support of civil authorities
FAA	Federal Aviation Administration (DOT)
FM	field manual (Army)
GCC	geographic combatant commander
GCE	ground combat element (MAGTF)
GPS	Global Positioning System
HD	homeland defense
HS	homeland security
IGO	intergovernmental organization
IO	information operations
IPB	intelligence preparation of the battlespace
ISR	intelligence, surveillance, and reconnaissance
ISRD	intelligence, surveillance, and reconnaissance division
J-2	intelligence directorate of a joint staff
J-3	operations directorate of a joint staff
J-4	logistics directorate of a joint staff
JACCE	joint air component coordination element
JAGIC	joint air-ground integration center
JAOC	joint air operations center
JAOP	joint air operations plan

JDDOC	joint deployment and distribution operations center
JFACC	joint force air component commander
JFC	joint force commander
JFE	joint fires element
JFLCC	joint force land component commander
JFMCC	joint force maritime component commander
JFSOCC	joint force special operations component commander
JIPCL	joint integrated prioritized collection list
JIPOE	joint intelligence preparation of the operational environment
JIPTL	joint integrated prioritized target list
JMC	joint movement center
JOA	joint operations area
JOC	joint operations center
JOPPA	joint operation planning process for air
JP	joint publication
JPRC	joint personnel recovery center
JSOACC	joint special operations air component commander
JSOTF	joint special operations task force
JTAC	joint terminal attack controller
JTCB	joint targeting coordination board
JTF	joint task force
JTWG	joint targeting working group
LNO	liaison officer
LOE	line of effort
LOO	line of operation
MAAP	master air attack plan
MACCS	Marine air command and control system
MAGTF	Marine air-ground task force
Marine TACC	Marine Corps tactical air command center
MARLE	Marine liaison element
MCRP	Marine Corps reference publication
MOC	maritime operations center
MOE	measure of effectiveness
MOP	measure of performance
NALE	naval and amphibious liaison element
Navy TACC	Navy tactical air control center
NCC	Navy component commander
NGO	nongovernmental organization
NORAD	North American Aerospace Defense Command
NTACS	Navy tactical air control system
NTTP	Navy tactics, techniques, and procedures

OCA	offensive counterair
OPCON	operational control
OPLAN	operation plan
OTC	officer in tactical command
PED	processing, exploitation, and dissemination
PNT	positioning, navigation, and timing
PR	personnel recovery
PRCC	personnel recovery coordination cell
RCT	rescue coordination team (Navy)
ROE	rules of engagement
ROZ	restricted operations zone
RSO	remote split operations
SCA	space coordinating authority
SD	strategy division
SIDO	senior intelligence duty officer
SOAGS	special operations air-ground system
SOF	special operations forces
SOLE	special operations liaison element
SORTIEALOT	sortie allotment message
SPINS	special instructions
TACON	tactical control
TACP	tactical air control party
TACS	theater air control system
TAGS	theater air-ground system
TAOC	tactical air operations center (USMC)
TBMCS	theater battle management core system
TET	targeting effects team
TNL	target nomination list
TPFDD	time-phased force and deployment data
TSOC	tactical special operations command
TST	time-sensitive target
UA	unmanned aircraft
UAS	unmanned aircraft system
USAF	United States Air Force
USC	United States Code
USCG	United States Coast Guard
USG	United States Government
USNORTHCOM	United States Northern Command
USPACOM	United States Pacific Command
USSOCOM	United States Special Operations Command
USSOUTHCOM	United States Southern Command

USSTRATCOM   United States Strategic Command
USTRANSCOM   United States Transportation Command

WMD   weapons of mass destruction

PART II–TERMS AND DEFINITIONS

air component coordination element. None. (Approved for removal from JP 1-02.)

air domain. The atmosphere, beginning at the Earth's surface, extending to the altitude where its effects upon operations become negligible. (JP 1-02. SOURCE: JP 3-30)

air expeditionary task force. A deployed numbered air force or command echelon immediately subordinate to a numbered air force provided as the United States Air Force component command committed to a joint operation. Also called **AETF.** (Approved for replacement of "air and space expeditionary task force" in JP 1-02.)

air operations center. The senior agency of the Air Force component commander that provides command and control of Air Force air and space operations and coordinates with other components and Services. Also called **AOC.** (Approved for replacement of "air and space operations center" in JP 1-02.)

air support request. A means to request preplanned and immediate close air support, air interdiction, air reconnaissance, surveillance, escort, helicopter airlift, and other aircraft missions. Also called **AIRSUPREQ.** (JP 1-02. SOURCE: JP 3-30)

air tasking order. A method used to task and disseminate to components, subordinate units, and command and control agencies projected sorties, capabilities and/or forces to targets and specific missions. Also called **ATO.** (Approved for incorporation into JP 1-02.)

allocation request. A daily message that provides an estimate of the total air effort, to identify any excess and joint force general support aircraft sorties, and to identify unfilled air requirements for preplanned missions. Also called **ALLOREQ.** (Approved for incorporation into JP 1-02.)

allotment. None. (Approved for removal from JP 1-02.)

centralized control. 1. In air defense, the control mode whereby a higher echelon makes direct target assignments to fire units. (JP 3-01) 2. In joint air operations, placing within one commander the responsibility and authority for planning, directing, and coordinating a military operation or group/category of operations. (JP 1-02. SOURCE: JP 3-30)

decentralized execution. Delegation of execution authority to subordinate commanders. (JP 1-02. SOURCE: JP 3-30)

flight. 1. In Navy and Marine Corps usage, a specified group of aircraft usually engaged in a common mission. 2. The basic tactical unit in the Air Force, consisting of four or more aircraft in two or more elements. 3. A single aircraft airborne on a nonoperational mission. (JP 1-02. SOURCE: JP 3-30)

joint air component coordination element. A general term for the liaison element that serves as the direct representative of the joint force air component commander for joint air operations. Also called **JACCE.** (JP 1-02. SOURCE: JP 3-30)

joint air operations. Air operations performed with air capabilities/forces made available by components in support of the joint force commander's operation or campaign objectives, or in support of other components of the joint force. (JP 1-02. SOURCE: JP 3-30)

joint air operations center. A jointly staffed facility established for planning, directing, and executing joint air operations in support of the joint force commander's operation or campaign objectives. Also called **JAOC.** (JP 1-02. SOURCE: JP 3-30)

joint air operations plan. A plan for a connected series of joint air operations to achieve the joint force commander's objectives within a given time and joint operational area. Also called **JAOP.** (JP 1-02. SOURCE: JP 3-30)

mission. 1. The task, together with the purpose, that clearly indicates the action to be taken and the reason therefore. (JP 3-0) 2. In common usage, especially when applied to lower military units, a duty assigned to an individual or unit; a task. (JP 3-0) 3. The dispatching of one or more aircraft to accomplish one particular task. (JP 1-02. SOURCE: JP 3-30)

reachback. The process of obtaining products, services, and applications, or forces, or equipment, or material from organizations that are not forward deployed. (JP 1-02. SOURCE: JP 3-30)

sortie. In air operations, an operational flight by one aircraft. (JP 1-02. SOURCE: JP 3-30)

sortie allotment message. The means by which the joint force commander allots excess sorties to meet requirements of subordinate commanders that are expressed in their air employment and/or allocation plan. Also called **SORTIEALOT.** (JP 1-02. SOURCE: JP 3-30)

tactical air support element. None. (Approved for removal from JP 1-02.)

traffic pattern. None. (Approved for removal from JP 1-02.)

unmanned aircraft. An aircraft that does not carry a human operator and is capable of flight with or without human remote control. Also called **UA.** (Approved for incorporation into JP 1-02.)

unmanned aircraft system. That system whose components include the necessary equipment, network, and personnel to control an unmanned aircraft. Also called **UAS.** (Approved for incorporation into JP 1-02 with JP 3-30 as the source JP.)

Intentionally Blank

JOINT DOCTRINE PUBLICATIONS HIERARCHY

JP 1
JOINT DOCTRINE
JP 1-0
PERSONNEL
JP 2-0
INTELLIGENCE
JP 3-0
OPERATIONS
JP 4-0
LOGISTICS
JP 5-0
PLANS
JP 6-0
COMMUNICATIONS SYSTEM

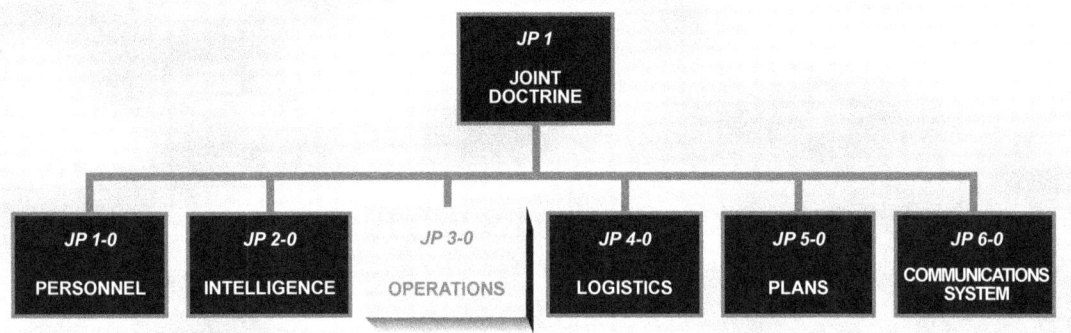

All joint publications are organized into a comprehensive hierarchy as shown in the chart above. **Joint Publication (JP) 3-30** is in the **Operations** series of joint doctrine publications. The diagram below illustrates an overview of the development process:

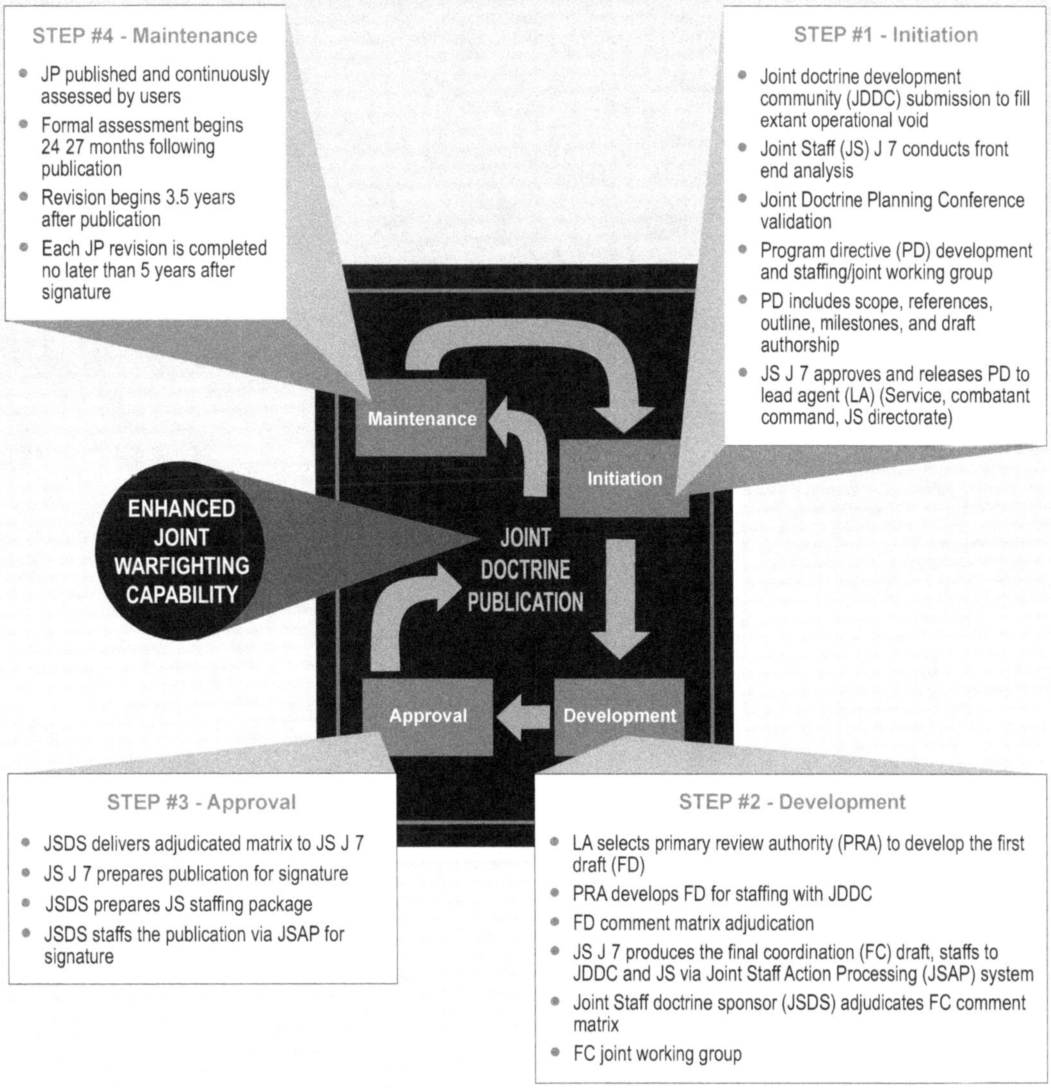

STEP #4 - Maintenance
JP published and continuously assessed by users
Formal assessment begins 24 27 months following publication
Revision begins 3.5 years after publication
Each JP revision is completed no later than 5 years after signature
STEP #1 - Initiation
Joint doctrine development community (JDDC) submission to fill extant operational void
Joint Staff (JS) J 7 conducts front end analysis
Joint Doctrine Planning Conference validation
Program directive (PD) development and staffing/joint working group
PD includes scope, references, outline, milestones, and draft authorship
JS J 7 approves and releases PD to lead agent (LA) (Service, combatant command, JS directorate)
Maintenance
Initiation
ENHANCED JOINT WARFIGHTING CAPABILITY
JOINT DOCTRINE PUBLICATION
Approval
Development
STEP #3 - Approval
JSDS delivers adjudicated matrix to JS J 7
JS J 7 prepares publication for signature
JSDS prepares JS staffing package
JSDS staffs the publication via JSAP for signature
STEP #2 - Development
LA selects primary review authority (PRA) to develop the first draft (FD)
PRA develops FD for staffing with JDDC
FD comment matrix adjudication
JS J 7 produces the final coordination (FC) draft, staffs to JDDC and JS via Joint Staff Action Processing (JSAP) system
Joint Staff doctrine sponsor (JSDS) adjudicates FC comment matrix
FC joint working group